DRUG EDUCATION LIBRARY

STEROIDS

by Jacqueline Adams

LUCENT BOOKS

An imprint of Thomson Gale, a part of The Thomson Corporation

THOMSON
━━━━━✦━━━━━ ™
GALE

Detroit • New York • San Francisco • San Diego • New Haven, Conn.
Waterville, Maine • London • Munich

Acknowledgments
For time spent answering my questions and/or reviewing portions of the manuscript, I am indebted to the following researchers: Shalender Bhasin, Don H. Catlin, Thomas D. Fahey, Caroline K. Hatton, Harrison G. Pope Jr., Thomas W. Storer, and Charles E. Yesalis.

I would like to thank Linn Goldberg for providing information on the ATLAS and ATHENA programs, Gregory E. White for his advice on natural performance enhancement, and Steve Courson and Donald M. Hooton Sr. for sharing their experiences.

For unfailing support that made this project possible, this book is dedicated to my husband, Donald K. Adams.

LIBRARY OF CONGRESS CATALOGING-IN-PUBLICATION DATA

Adams, Jacqueline, 1969–
  Steroids / by Jacqueline Adams.
    p. cm. — (Drug education library)
  Includes bibliographical references and index.
  ISBN 1-56006-917-1 (hard cover : alk. paper) 1. Steroids. I. Title. II. Series.
  RC1230.A33 2006
  362.29—dc22
                                                                    2005019454

CONTENTS

Foreword

The development of drugs and drug use in America is a cultural paradox. On the one hand, strong, potentially dangerous drugs provide people with relief from numerous physical and psychological ailments. Sedatives like Valium counter the effects of anxiety; steroids treat severe burns, anemia, and some forms of cancer; morphine provides quick pain relief. On the other hand, many drugs (sedatives, steroids, and morphine among them) are consistently misused or abused. Millions of Americans struggle each year with drug addictions that overpower their ability to think and act rationally. Researchers often link drug abuse to criminal activity, traffic accidents, domestic violence, and suicide.

These harmful effects seem obvious today. Newspaper articles, medical papers, and scientific studies have highlighted the myriad problems drugs and drug use can cause. Yet, there was a time when many of the drugs now known to be harmful were actually believed to be beneficial. Cocaine, for example, was once hailed as a great cure, used to treat everything from nausea and weakness to colds and asthma. Developed in Europe during the 1880s, cocaine spread quickly to the United States where manufacturers made it the primary ingredient in such everyday substances as cough medicines, lozenges, and tonics. Likewise, heroin, an opium derivative, became a popular painkiller during the late nineteenth century. Doctors and patients flocked to American drugstores to buy heroin, described as the optimal cure for even the worst coughs and chest pains.

As more people began using these drugs, though, doctors, legislators, and the public at large began to realize that they were more damaging than beneficial. After years of using heroin as a painkiller, for example, patients began asking their doctors for larger and stronger doses. Cocaine users reported dangerous side effects, including hallucinations and wild mood shifts. As a result, the U.S. government initiated more stringent regulation of many powerful and addictive drugs, and in some cases outlawed them entirely.

A drug's legal status is not always indicative of how dangerous it is, however. Some drugs known to have harmful effects can be purchased legally in the United States and elsewhere. Nicotine, a key ingredient in cigarettes, is known to be highly addictive. In an effort to meet their bodies' demands for nicotine, smokers expose themselves to lung cancer, emphysema, and other life-threatening conditions. Despite these risks, nicotine is legal almost everywhere.

Other drugs that cannot be purchased or sold legally are the subject of much debate regarding their effects on physical and mental health. Marijuana, sometimes described as a gateway drug that leads users to other drugs, cannot legally be used, grown, or sold in this country. However, some research suggests that marijuana is neither addictive nor a gateway drug and that it might actually benefit cancer and AIDS patients by reducing pain and encouraging failing appetites. Despite these findings and occasional legislative attempts to change the drug's status, marijuana remains illegal.

The Drug Education Library examines the paradox of drugs and drug use in America by focusing on some of the most commonly used and abused drugs or categories of drugs available today. By discussing objectively the many types of drugs, their intended purposes, their effects (both planned and unplanned), and the controversies surrounding them, the books in this series provide readers with an understanding of the complex role drugs and drug use play in American society. Informative sidebars, annotated bibliographies, and organizations to contact lists highlight the text and provide young readers with many opportunities for further discussion and research.

AN ONGOING SCANDAL

When *Sports Illustrated* ran a three-part series on the use of drugs in sports in 1969, it quoted Robert Kerlan, former physician for the Los Angeles Dodgers, as saying that "the excessive and secretive use of drugs is likely to become a major athletic scandal, one that will shake public confidence in many sports."[1] His prediction proved remarkably accurate in the opening years of the twenty-first century, when elite athletes in several sports were implicated in a well-publicized scandal involving use of anabolic steroids and other performance-enhancing drugs.

Although they were developed for medical use in the 1930s, synthetic anabolic steroids, all derivatives of the male hormone testosterone, were later adopted by athletes for their muscle-building properties. Beginning in the 1970s, sporting organizations banned anabolic steroids due to concerns over fair competition and health risks. According to testimony from athletes, secretive anabolic steroid use became widespread in many sports.

As Kerlan predicted, the situation erupted into "a major athletic scandal." After authorities raided the Bay Area Laboratory

Cooperative (BALCO) in 2003, four men were charged with supplying anabolic steroids and other illegal drugs to athletes. The athletes implicated included track-and-field world champions and National Football League and Major League Baseball (MLB) stars. Some of these MLB players had previously denied using anabolic steroids.

The BALCO investigation set off a chain reaction of events that kept anabolic steroids in the headlines for many months. MLB, under pressure from politicians and the media, passed a stricter drug-testing policy in January 2005.

In his 2005 tell-all book *Juiced,* former MLB slugger Jose Canseco claims that steroid use is rife in professional baseball.

Greek weight lifter Leonidas Sampanis was stripped of his bronze medal after testing positive for steroids during the 2004 Olympics.

In his book released in February 2005, retired MLB player Jose Canseco claimed that while he was playing, anabolic steroids were as acceptable as a cup of coffee. He named other elite players, including Mark McGwire and Rafael Palmeiro, who he said used the drugs. In March 2005 Congress subpoenaed Canseco, McGwire, Palmeiro, and other MLB players to testify about anabolic steroids before the House Government Reform Committee. McGwire, who broke the single-season home run record in 1998, refused to answer questions about his alleged anabolic steroid use, saying, "I'm not here to talk about the past."[2]

Palmeiro said, "I have never used steroids. Period. I do not know how to say it any more clearly than that."[3] A few months later, he became the seventh MLB player to test positive for anabolic steroids under the new drug-testing policy. He received a ten-day suspension but denied that he had knowingly used the drugs. Some congressmen felt that the incident highlighted the need for a federal law requiring stricter drug testing with harsher penalties in professional sports.

Also as Kerlan predicted, the scandal shook public confidence. MLB fans who wondered whether records and performances were drug-assisted pointed to players who had suddenly become more muscular and to the increase in home runs starting in the late 1990s as reasons for suspicion. When the number of home runs dropped nearly 7 percent in the first half of 2005, debate raged over whether the new drug-testing policy was the reason. Sports reporter Jack Curry wrote, "It is a state of mind that has now become part of the game. Players, managers, fans and reporters can watch a batter crush a ball 450 feet (137m) or hammer a ball to the opposite field and, even if the only evidence is their eyes, they will be tempted to issue a verdict on whether the home run was clean or tainted."[4]

Shaken public confidence also affects drug-free athletes who must compete under a cloud of suspicion. While MLB players lament that every home run seems to raise doubts in the minds of fans, athletes in other sports find themselves in a similar situation. Don H. Catlin, head of the Olympic drug-testing lab at the University of California, Los Angeles, has conversed with drug-free Olympic athletes over this "very painful issue." He relates, "They're terribly frustrated because athletes who do well end up getting accused of taking a drug."[5]

Meanwhile, the publicity has heightened concern over another affected group—the growing number of teens who are turning to anabolic steroids. Professional athletes implicated in doping scandals have come under increasing fire for their failure as role models. In his 2004 State of the Union address, President George W. Bush said:

> To help children make right choices, they need good examples. Athletics play such an important role in society, but, unfortunately, some in professional sports are not setting much of an example. The use of performance-enhancing drugs like steroids in baseball, football, and other sports is dangerous, and it sends the wrong message that there are shortcuts to accomplishment, and that performance is more important than character. So tonight I call on team owners, union representatives, coaches, and players to take the lead, to send the right signal, to get tough, and to get rid of steroids now.[6]

Concern over the effects on college and high school athletes was one reason Congress conducted the 2005 hearings. Young users often see only the success of professional athletes who use anabolic steroids, and they may not consider, or even be aware of, the possible physical and psychological side effects. Donald M. Hooton Sr., who attributes his seventeen-year-old son's suicide to anabolic steroid use, testified before Congress, "I believe the poor example being set by professional athletes is a major catalyst fueling the high usage of steroids amongst our kids. Our kids look up to these guys. They want to do the things the pros do to be successful."[7] In addition, some teen nonathletes, both male and female, take anabolic steroids in an effort to attain the lean, muscular look of today's models, musicians, and movie stars.

When Kerlan made his comments back in 1969, he said, "Somebody should speak out on this subject, and speak out strongly."[8] Today, in the midst of ongoing scandal, many voices speak out on the problem of performance-enhancing drugs, while sporting organizations struggle to regain public confidence.

Chapter 1

THE QUEST FOR STRENGTH

At the mention of anabolic steroids, most people think of illegal drugs taken for performance enhancement. Twenty-first-century headlines are filled with scandals involving athletes who failed drug tests and reports of growing numbers of young users.

Because synthetic anabolic steroids have become infamous as drugs of abuse, many fail to realize that researchers originally developed them for treating medical problems. These drugs soon spread far beyond their intended use.

Early History

The body naturally produces anabolic steroids, including the primary anabolic steroid, testosterone. These hormones have androgenic, or masculinizing, effects because they are responsible for the development of the male reproductive organs and secondary male characteristics, such as growth of facial and body hair. They also have anabolic, or tissue-building, effects, including increased muscle size and strength.

Thousands of years before anabolic steroids were officially discovered, people noted what happened when the testes, which produce testosterone, were removed. They discovered that castrating an animal caused it to become less aggressive and lose its male characteristics. Through the centuries, castration was used not only to domesticate animals but also on humans as punishment, to create eunuchs to guard harems or serve as priests, and to prevent the voices of choirboys from deepening.

Scientists were not in agreement as to how the testes controlled these changes. Some suggested that the testes and other organs regulated bodily functions by secreting substances into the blood, but most believed that the testes worked through the nervous system. With a simple experiment in 1849, German professor of medicine Arnold A. Berthold endeavored to find the answer to this age-old puzzle. Berthold castrated four roosters and transplanted a testis

This seventeenth-century illustration depicts the castration of an involuntary patient. For many centuries, castration served as a common form of punishment.

into the abdomen of two of them. The roosters that did not receive the implants became less aggressive and their combs and wattles shrank—the usual results of castration. The roosters with an implanted testis maintained their appearance and behavior. Berthold concluded that the testes, which no longer had nerve connections, must regulate bodily characteristics by secreting a substance into the bloodstream.

In 1889 seventy-two-year-old French physiologist Charles-Édouard Brown-Séquard announced that he had conducted an experiment in which he had injected himself with liquid extracts of dog and guinea pig testicles. He claimed that this treatment rejuvenated him, improving his physical and mental health. Most scientists believe that Brown-Séquard's findings were a result of the placebo effect, or the power of suggestion, but his claims prompted researchers around the world to experiment with testicular extracts as cures for problems ranging from migraines to cancer.

In 1905 British physiologist Ernest Starling gave the name *hormones* to the function-controlling chemicals secreted by the body. For the next three decades, scientists worked to identify the male hormone secreted by the testes, believing it had great potential for medical use.

The Discovery of Testosterone
Some physicians followed Brown-Séquard's lead by injecting testicular extracts into themselves or into patients. Beginning in 1912, other physicians went further, transplanting testes from human donors and from animals into human males as a cure for impotence and disorders as diverse as asthma, epilepsy, tuberculosis, and paranoia. This practice continued throughout the 1920s. Although many patients reported improved health, the medical community eventually concluded that this was the result of the placebo effect and that the transplants were ineffective.

Meanwhile, other scientists worked to isolate the hormones responsible for producing male characteristics. In

1935 they isolated the principal male hormone, testosterone, which is one of the group of organic compounds called steroids. Plants and animals naturally produce hundreds of different types of steroids. In humans, the adrenal glands, the ovaries of females, and the testes of males produce hormones that are steroids. Testosterone is produced primarily by the testes, although the adrenal glands of both males and females also produce small amounts.

Because of the difficulty and expense of extracting natural testosterone, researchers worked to develop synthetic versions. In August 1935 two different research teams, one led by Leopold Ruzicka in Switzerland and one by Adolf Butenandt in Germany, discovered a way to produce synthetic testosterone from cholesterol. For their work on hormones, both men were awarded the 1939 Nobel Prize for chemistry.

Researchers learned that the body converts testosterone to other anabolic steroids, with the testosterone molecule having the potential to be converted into six hundred different steroids. They named this family of steroids *androgens*, meaning "producing male characteristics." By manipulating the structure of the testosterone molecule, researchers eventually developed more than one hundred synthetic anabolic steroids.

A Muscle-Building Compound

While researchers were working to isolate and synthesize androgens, Charles D. Kochakian of the University of Rochester conducted experiments that indicated that these compounds have anabolic, or tissue-building, properties. This raised the possibility that the new synthetic drugs could be used to treat patients suffering from wasting conditions.

By 1937 researchers were experimenting with medical applications for synthetic testosterone. They used it as replacement therapy for men with hypogonadism, a condition in which sufferers experience loss of muscle, beard and body hair, and sexual function because their bodies do not produce enough of the hormone. Beginning in the late 1930s the

After the first transplant of a human testicle in Philadelphia in 1912, the reported success led other surgeons to take up this practice. Leo L. Stanley, the physician at San Quentin prison in California, began transplanting testes removed from executed inmates in 1918. The transplants were so popular that he did not have enough donors and began using ram, goat, deer, and boar testes in 1920. Patients suffering from problems as diverse as asthma, epilepsy, and senility underwent the operation hoping for relief.

Serge Voronoff, a Russian-born surgeon who practiced in Paris, believed that the slowing of hormone secretions caused aging and that he could rejuvenate humans by transplanting slices of chimpanzee and baboon testes. After experimenting on many animals, Voronoff performed his first "monkeygland" transplant on a human in 1920. The surgery became so popular that thousands of men around the world had received these glands by the early 1930s. Although Voronoff believed in his results, the scientific community was unconvinced. The practice ended in the 1930s.

drugs were used successfully to treat psychiatric disorders involving depression. In the 1940s doctors began using anabolic steroids to treat burns and battle wounds, to help patients recover from surgery, and to treat breast cancers related to the female hormone estrogen in the hopes that testosterone would counteract estrogen and shrink the tumor. After World War II doctors treated emaciated Nazi concentration camp survivors with testosterone for its muscle-building effects. An obstacle to use in female patients was the androgenic

effect of these steroids. They caused females to develop facial and body hair, a deepened voice, and an enlarged clitoris.

Scientists struggled to develop synthetic versions of testosterone that would build muscle without masculinizing patients. Although they were able to reduce the androgenic effects, they never succeeded in eliminating them. Because of this, the full name of this class of drugs is anabolic-androgenic steroids, although they are commonly called anabolic steroids.

Other groups of steroids do not have anabolic properties. In fact, the steroids known as glucocorticoids, which are produced by the adrenals, are catabolic, meaning they break down tissue. One of these, cortisone, was isolated in 1935, and a synthetic version was first used in 1948 to successfully treat severe rheumatoid arthritis. The synthetic versions, called corticosteroids, are the steroids most commonly used in medicine. Besides arthritis treatment, corticosteroids are prescribed for asthma, lupus, allergies, inflammation associated with injuries, and other problems.

Another group of steroids without anabolic properties includes the female hormones estrogen and progesterone. These steroids are primarily produced by the ovaries, but the testes of males and the adrenals of both sexes also produce small amounts. Female hormones also have synthetic counterparts that doctors prescribe for birth control, relief of premenstrual syndrome, and as replacement therapy when the body's natural production of these hormones decreases.

From Medical Use to Performance-Enhancing Drug

While doctors explored medical uses for the newly discovered drugs, others considered the possibility that anabolic steroids might enhance athletic performance. The first-known use of anabolic steroids in sports was not in a human but rather in a horse. In 1941, at age eighteen, the trotter Holloway had lost much of his speed and stamina. At age nineteen, after a training program that included implantation of testosterone pellets, he set a new trotting record.

A popular 1945 book, *The Male Hormone*, promoted the idea that human athletes could benefit from testosterone use. Its author, Paul de Kruif, reported that testosterone could restore productivity and improve athletic performance. He wrote, "We know how both the St. Louis Cardinals and the St. Louis Browns have won championships supercharged by vitamins. It would be interesting to watch the productive power of an industry or a professional group (of athletes) that would try a systematic supercharge with testosterone."[9]

The first reports of human athletes using anabolic steroids for performance enhancement come from the early 1950s. West Coast bodybuilders experimented with testosterone during this time. When the Russian weight-lifting team won seven medals at the 1952 Olympic Games in Helsinki, the U.S. team coach, Bob Hoffman, alleged that the Russians were using testosterone. The U.S. team physician, John Ziegler, confirmed this suspicion two years later at the 1954

A member of the U.S. weight-lifting team competes at the 1954 Heavyweight World Championship, where the Americans lost to the steroid-enhanced Russian team.

To prepare mentally for Olympic competition, athletes in ancient Greece drank a mixture of wine and strychnine or ate hallucinogenic mushrooms. Greek distance runners ate sesame seeds in the belief that these would increase endurance. Roman gladiators fought fatigue with stimulants such as caffeine and strychnine.

Nineteenth-century athletes commonly sought to enhance performance with drugs such as caffeine, cocaine, strychnine, opium, and heroin.

By the 1950s athletes were using amphetamines, a type of drug that stimulates the central nervous system, to increase energy and endurance.

Besides anabolic steroids, modern athletes have turned to a variety of hormones in their quest for victory. Some strength athletes use human growth hormone for its anabolic effects, but it results in irreversible disfigurement by causing the bones as well as the muscles to grow. In recent years some athletes have begun using insulin to promote muscle growth. When asked about the dangers of this new trend, Charles E. Yesalis of Penn State University told a Reuters reporter, "It's called death if you overdose with insulin. That's no secret."

In this ancient Greek relief, athletes compete in a ball game. Greek athletes routinely used performance-enhancing substances.

World Weightlifting Championships in Vienna. "I got to be friends with the Russian team doctor, and one night we went out on the town. We had a few drinks, and he told me some members of his team were using testosterone."[10]

When Ziegler returned to the United States, he put testosterone to the test by taking it himself and giving it to Hoffman and a few East Coast weight lifters. Although they experienced the drug's anabolic effects in the form of increased muscle size and strength, Ziegler was concerned about the androgenic effects, which included prostate enlargement. The problem seemed solved in 1958, when Ciba Pharmaceutical Company released Dianabol, one of the modified steroids that were developed in an effort to reduce androgenic effects so the drugs could be used for medical purposes.

Ziegler began a training program with three weight lifters from the York Barbell Club, owned by Hoffman. These weight lifters took Dianabol and trained with isometric contraction, in which they worked their muscles against immovable objects. As the three made great gains in muscle size and strength, they drew the attention of other lifters, who wanted to know the secret of their success. Hoffman responded by publishing an article in a fitness magazine describing their training with isometric contraction. Other lifters followed the training program but did not get the same results. As the three continued to excel and became national champions, others learned the rest of their secret—Dianabol. The news that anabolic steroids could lead to athletic success spread through the weight-lifting world and to many other sports.

Olympic Athletes Embrace Steroids

The rivalry between America and the Soviet Union during the Cold War played a role in encouraging anabolic steroid use. American team physicians and athletes believed that synthetic testosterone gave their rivals from the Soviet-bloc nations an advantage. Ziegler stated his belief that the Soviets would use their success in sports as an international publicity trick to promote the superiority of the Communist system. By the 1960 Olympics, American weight lifters had joined the Russians in using anabolic steroids. Track-and-field throwers (shot put, discus, javelin, and hammer) soon followed.

By the late 1960s weight lifters and throwers were taking much higher doses of anabolic steroids. Athletes began taking combinations of different anabolic steroids, a practice known as stacking, in the belief that this would produce greater muscle gains than using one steroid at a time. Although the International Olympic Committee (IOC) banned certain drugs in 1967 to protect the health of athletes and to ensure fair competition, steroids were not on the list. Because of conflicting results of early scientific studies, many physicians believed the drugs did not enhance athletic performance. Another reason steroids were not listed was that the IOC would have had no way to enforce a ban since no test for these substances existed at the time.

By the 1968 Olympic Games in Mexico City, anabolic steroid use had spread to sprinters, hurdlers, and middle-distance runners. Decathlon athlete Tom Waddell stated that he believed a third of all U.S. track-and-field athletes had used steroids at the training camp to prepare for these Olympics. Dave Maggard of the U.S. track-and-field team said, "Are anabolic steroids widely used by Olympic weight men? Let me put it this way. If they had come into the village the day before competition and said we have just found a new test that will catch anyone who has used steroids, you would have had an awful lot of people dropping out of events because of instant muscle pulls."[11]

Although anabolic steroids were not banned, many athletes used them in secret rather than admit that performance-enhancing drugs had contributed to their success. Others saw no ethical problems with using the drugs. In 1971 American weight-lifting champion Ken Patera explained publicly why he was looking forward to competing against Russian super-heavyweight Vasily Alexeev in the 1972 Olympic Games:

"Last year the only difference between me and him was I couldn't afford his drug bill. Now I can. When I hit Munich I'll weigh in at about 340 [154kg], or maybe 350 [159kg]. Then we'll see which are better, his steroids or mine."[12]

At the 1972 Olympics, Jay Sylvester of the U.S. track-and-field team took an unofficial poll that revealed how widespread steroid use had become. Sixty-eight percent of the track-and-field athletes present told him they had used anabolic steroids in their training. By the 1990s use had been reported in a long list of Olympic sports, including swimming, cycling, wrestling, handball, soccer, and winter sports.

Female Athletes Turn to Male Hormones

While male athletes led the way in anabolic steroid use, female Olympians soon followed. The first reports of female athletes using male hormones came from the German Democratic Republic (GDR). Beginning in 1966 the GDR carried on a systematic sports-doping program in which scientists gave anabolic steroids to thousands of athletes—male and female, adolescent and adult—every year. This occurred in secret so that the rest of the world would not know that the success of the GDR athletes was drug assisted. The Western world learned the details only after the fall of the GDR, when several classified documents came to light. Similar programs may have existed in other Communist-bloc nations.

Doctors working for the government program began giving the drugs to females in preparation for the 1968 Olympic Games. Over the next few years they increased the dosages to achieve greater results, but this also increased the masculinizing side effects. By the 1976 Olympics, these side effects had become so obvious that journalists asked the East German coach why his female swimmers' voices were so deep. He said simply, "We have come here to swim, not to sing."[13]

Since the female body naturally produces only small amounts of testosterone, female athletes who take anabolic steroids may experience more noticeable gains in muscle size and strength

Gold medalist Andrea Pollack was one of several athletes suspected of steroid use during the 1976 Olympics.

than males who take these drugs. The athletic success of the East German women encouraged the spread of steroid use to women in other Eastern-bloc nations (allies of the Communist government of the Soviet Union) and, by the 1970s, to women in Western nations. The rise to Olympic success—and the large number of positive drug tests—of Chinese women during the 1990s has led to speculation that China may be carrying on a systematic sports-doping program. Adding to the suspicion is the fact that former East German coaches began working in China after the fall of the GDR.

Spread Through Professional Sports

Anabolic steroid use soon expanded from Olympic sports to professional sports. These drugs may have infiltrated professional football via Alvin Roy, a Baton Rouge gym owner who had been an assistant coach for the U.S. Olympic weightlifting team. In 1963 the San Diego Chargers hired Roy as the first professional football strength coach. Players reported that he gave Dianabol to most of the team. "He did not say that the pills were steroids, only that taking them would help us assimilate protein, 'the building blocks of muscle,'" said offensive guard Ron Mix. After taking the drugs for five weeks, another player sought advice from a neighbor who was a physician. The physician advised him against taking the drugs for an extended time. Mix said, "When the rest of us heard that, most stopped. But for many, the prospect of being stronger was too intoxicating, the hope for an advantage too enticing, the fear of failure too great; and they continued."[14]

Use spread to other teams and was reportedly common in the National Football League (NFL) by the late 1970s. Although spokesmen for the NFL and the NFL Players Association denied that there was a problem, players told a different story. "Steroids are very, very accepted in the NFL," said Pat Donovan, a Dallas Cowboys offensive lineman who retired in 1983. "In my last five or six years it ran as high as 60 to 70 percent on the Cowboys on the offensive and defensive lines."[15] Players from other teams gave estimates ranging from 40 to 90 percent of all players.

The drugs have been reported in other professional sports, including rugby and wrestling. Use in bodybuilding is so prevalent that many believe it is impossible to compete at the professional level without taking them. In 2002, when Ken Caminiti became the first retired Major League Baseball (MLB) player to admit that he had used anabolic steroids, he claimed that half the players took them. Retired player Jose Canseco went further, estimating use at 85 percent of players. A *USA Today* poll that year revealed that although most MLB players believed that some players used steroids, they thought that Caminiti's and Canseco's numbers were exaggerated.

College Athletes Follow the Professionals

Anabolic steroid use in college sports followed the pattern of the professionals. Steve Courson, former offensive lineman

for the Pittsburgh Steelers and Tampa Bay Buccaneers, recalls the casual attitude toward anabolic steroids he encountered as a sophomore at the University of South Carolina in 1974. When an assistant coach suggested he try anabolic steroids, Courson asked one of the team physicians about the drugs. "This team doctor asked no questions. He simply took my blood pressure and handed me a prescription for 30 five-milligram tablets of Dianabol."[16] The university paid for the prescription, according to Courson.

The National Collegiate Athletic Association (NCAA) officially outlawed anabolic steroids in 1973, but it did not begin testing for the drugs until 1986. That year, more than twenty football players who tested positive were banned from playing in postseason bowl games.

Every four years since 1989, the NCAA research staff has taken an anonymous survey to learn about substance use in college athletes. The first survey revealed that 4.9 percent of all athletes used anabolic steroids. The numbers dropped to 1.1 percent in 1997 and climbed to 1.4 percent with the most recent survey, taken in 2001.

The highest percentage of anabolic steroid use in men's sports in the 2001 survey was in water polo, with 5.0 percent of athletes responding that they used the drugs. Rifle was second (4.2 percent), followed by football (3.0 percent). The highest use among female college athletes was in lacrosse (1.6 percent), followed by swimming (1.3 percent).

Young Users

Perhaps the most disturbing revelation for researchers conducting the study was the age at which anabolic steroid use begins. Some 57.2 percent of users said they began taking the drugs when they were in high school or younger. Rumors of high school use date back to 1959, when members of a football team were reportedly given Dianabol by a Texas physician. In the early 1960s a high school football team physician secretly gave anabolic steroids to players as research

After former San Diego Padres player Ken Caminiti retired from baseball, he admitted to using anabolic steroids during his professional career.

for a pharmaceutical company. When coaches from other teams complained, the program was stopped. In 1965 H. Kay Dooley of Pomona, California, conducted a study in which he gave three different brands of anabolic steroids to tenth- and eleventh-grade high school football players. He reported that these players experienced increased muscle size with no undesirable side effects, but his study was not controlled enough to reach definite conclusions.

Use spread from football to other high school sports and to students who were not athletes but who believed the drugs would improve their appearance. The annual Monitoring the Future Survey conducted by the University of Michigan revealed that an increasing number of high school students in the United States used steroids throughout the 1990s. In 2003 the number decreased slightly but still represented an

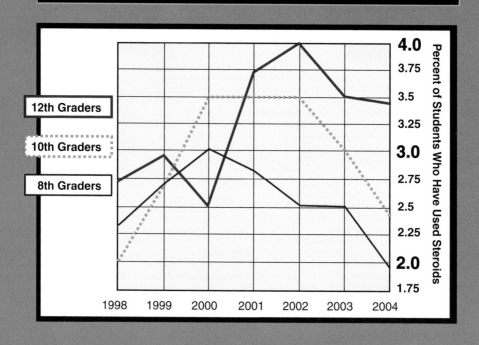

ANABOLIC-ANDROGENIC STEROID USE AMONG 8TH, 10TH, AND 12TH GRADERS IN THE UNITED STATES

Percent of Students Who Have Used Steroids

estimated three hundred thousand users in grades eight through twelve. Surveys taken in Canada, South Africa, England, Sweden, and Australia during the 1990s revealed high school user percentages similar to those in the United States.

Methods and Motives

Congress addressed the growing problem by passing the Anabolic Steroid Control Act of 1990, which made anabolic steroids a controlled substance. First-time possession could carry a penalty of up to a year in prison and a minimum fine of one thousand dollars. Although this made it difficult for doctors or pharmacists to provide anabolic steroids for performance enhancement, most users were already getting these drugs illegally on the black market rather than by prescription. On the street, anabolic steroids are referred to by slang terms such as *juice, gym candy, pumpers, stackers*, and *weight trainers.*

The most common ways athletes take anabolic steroids are by mouth or by injection, but the drugs also come in the form of creams, skin patches, or nasal sprays. Users usually take anabolic steroids in cycles of four to twelve weeks or longer, stop for a while, and then begin another cycle. Some users never go off cycle. *Pyramiding* is the process of starting a cycle with a low dose, increasing the dose until the middle of the cycle, and then gradually reducing it until the end. Users believe this process gives their bodies time to adjust to high doses (although this has not been scientifically proven) and makes detection by a drug test after the cycle less likely.

Users sometimes take other types of drugs along with anabolic steroids. Such a combination, called an array, may include other performance-enhancing drugs, such as stimulants and human growth hormone, and drugs intended to counteract the side effects of anabolic steroid use. Examples include antiestrogens to prevent breast development in male users and human chorionic gonadotropin to prevent the testes from shrinking.

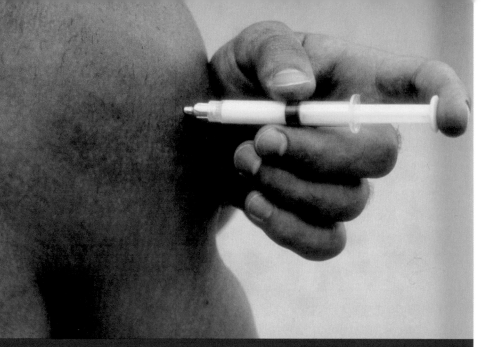

Anabolic steroids give athletes a strong competitive advantage, increasing muscle size and strength.

Anabolic steroids have spread far beyond their intended medical uses to groups who turn to them for a variety of reasons. Although the number of users is unknown, one survey estimates that there are more than 1 million current or former users in the United States alone. Whereas strength athletes use anabolic steroids to build muscle, endurance athletes take the drugs to help them recover more quickly between workouts. A growing group, which includes actors, musicians, models, and high school students, take these drugs to improve their appearance. Some bodyguards, construction workers, bouncers, policemen, and soldiers believe anabolic steroids will enhance their job performance.

Despite the seeming benefits, doctors have warned for years about the dangers of anabolic steroid abuse. Many users did not take the warnings seriously because some of these same doctors asserted that anabolic steroids did not build muscle and that any weight gains users experienced were the result of water retention or the power of suggestion. Researchers who later reopened the issue discovered the true link between anabolic steroids and athletic performance.

Chapter 2

Use and Abuse of a Muscle-Building Drug

During the 1960s and 1970s, when anabolic steroid use was sweeping through sport after sport, researchers conducted studies to determine how these drugs affect athletic performance. Although some studies showed increased muscle size and strength in subjects who used anabolic steroids, others did not. The conflicting results led many physicians to conclude that anabolic steroid use does not build muscle.

This position conflicted with the testimony of athletes, as Shalender Bhasin of the University of California, Los Angeles, learned when he began his career in the 1980s. He asked, "How could athletes and recreational bodybuilders and sports medicine physicians believe so fervently that these compounds have anabolic effects—and that was consistent with the widespread, growing abuse of these compounds—and how could the academic community have the completely opposite view of it?"[17] Bhasin and other researchers reexamined the issue. Their search for answers not only revealed the true effects of anabolic steroids on the body but also renewed interest in finding medical applications for these drugs.

The Voice of Experience

Athletes who experimented with anabolic steroids in the 1950s quickly experienced significant gains in muscle size and strength. In the years that followed, bodybuilders attained physiques that were much more muscular than those of bodybuilders in the presteroid era. Weight lifters, football players, and other strength athletes reported increases in muscle mass and in the amount of weight they could lift. Track-and-field athletes believed that anabolic steroids were responsible for the strength gains that allowed them to put the shot or throw the discus, hammer, or javelin farther.

Although the GDR kept its sports-doping program hidden from the rest of the world, its doctors recorded the performance improvements that GDR athletes experienced when taking anabolic steroids. These improvements were especially significant in adolescent and female athletes. In the first documented case of a female athlete using anabolic steroids, GDR doctors reported that she could put the shot two meters [7ft] farther after taking the drugs for only eleven weeks in 1968. In 1977, Manfred Höppner, the deputy director and chief physician of the GDR's Sports Medical Service, wrote, "The positive value of anabolic steroids for the development of a top performance is undoubted." He listed performance gains that male and female GDR athletes had made in various sporting events, and said, "From our experiences made so far it can be concluded that women have the greatest advantage from treatments with anabolic hormones with respect to their performance in sports. . . . Especially high is the performance-supporting effect following the first administration of anabolic hormones, especially with junior athletes."[18]

After stricter drug-testing controls were put into effect in 1989, the world's top performances declined in most women's events and in men's throwing events. Some observers believed this was an indication that earlier top performances were drug assisted.

Widespread Confusion

Meanwhile, based on the results of early studies, some researchers asserted that anabolic steroids were ineffective for performance enhancement. The lack of scientific evidence caused much debate in the 1960s. Since many athletes did not believe physicians' claims that anabolic steroids failed to build muscle, they also did not believe these physicians' claims that the drugs caused dangerous side effects. Adding to the confusion was the fact that no sporting organization had yet banned anabolic steroids. Dave Maggard, a University of California track team coach and a former Olympic shot putter, expressed his frustration in 1969: "What I wish is that some reputable scientific group would really study certain

Russian shot putter Irina Korzhanenko was stripped of her gold medal after failing a drug test at the 2004 Summer Olympics.

Offensive lineman Steve Courson of the Pittsburgh Steelers acknowledged the performance-enhancing effects he experienced while taking steroids.

drugs and tell us yes or no as to whether they are effective, and yes or no as to whether they are dangerous. Then I'd like to see the NCAA, the AAU, and the U.S. Olympic Committee and all the conferences go ahead and put us straight—tell all of us to either use the drugs, or don't."[19]

Even after sporting organizations banned anabolic steroids, confusion prevailed over the effectiveness and health consequences of these drugs. In 1977 the American College of Sports Medicine (ACSM) declared in a position statement that anabolic steroids do not enhance athletic performance. Former NFL offensive lineman Steve Courson expressed his reaction to such claims:

> Anyone who used them knew what a load of shinola that was. It was evident to me—and to anyone who observed me over a month's time—that these things worked remarkably well. Nor did I see any damaging health effects in myself or my peers. Perhaps if guys were dropping like flies in practice, I might have rethought my position. But back then there seemed to be only enormous benefits and few, if any, drawbacks.[20]

The ACSM changed its position in 1984, but by then the medical community had lost credibility with athletes who had experienced the performance-enhancing effects of anabolic steroids.

Reexamining the Question

In the 1980s researchers reviewed the earlier studies and identified several flaws responsible for the conflicting results. By neglecting to control the diet of study subjects or by using small doses of anabolic steroids, some studies failed to recreate the conditions under which athletes train on steroids. Some studies used subjects who were inexperienced with weight training. Since inexperienced people usually make much greater gains when they first begin weight training, whether or not they use anabolic steroids, this factor could obscure the differences in results between study subjects given anabolic steroids and subjects given a placebo. Most studies lasted only a few weeks, which may not have been long enough to show the true effects on inexperienced subjects.

Studies are also limited by ethical concerns. Some athletes take anabolic steroids in potentially dangerous doses or in combinations that no researcher could in good conscience give to study subjects, so studies cannot re-create

the experiences of these athletes. The irreversible masculinizing effects are another concern. Since researchers consider it
unethical to give anabolic steroids to women and children,
studies were limited to adult male subjects. Little was known
about these drugs' effects on women and children until after
the fall of the GDR in 1990. Formerly classified documents
detailing the government's sports-doping program revealed
not only severe side effects in women and children but also
the great increases in athletic performance.

Ethical concerns still apply, but researchers who reexamined
the link between anabolic steroids and athletic performance
were able to overcome some of the other problems of earlier
studies. A 1996 study by Bhasin and his colleagues used only
subjects who were experienced weight lifters and divided them
into four groups. Two groups were given testosterone, but
only one of these groups exercised during the study. The other
two groups were given a placebo they thought was testosterone, and one placebo group exercised. This ten-week study,
which was longer than most earlier studies, controlled subjects' diets and types of exercise and used a dose of testosterone higher than that used in previous studies.

The group that took testosterone and exercised showed
much greater gains in muscle size and strength than the other
three groups. The group that took testosterone but did not
exercise gained more muscle mass and almost as much muscle strength as the placebo group that exercised. This and
other studies have led most researchers to agree that anabolic
steroids, when taken along with a proper diet, increase muscle size and strength.

How Anabolic Steroids Build Muscle

Researchers hypothesize that anabolic steroids trigger these
changes by increasing protein synthesis in muscle cells. Hormones and other chemical messengers relay instructions
when they bind to receptor sites on cells. Anabolic steroids
bind to testosterone receptors on cells and send a signal for

HOW STEROIDS WORK IN THE BODY

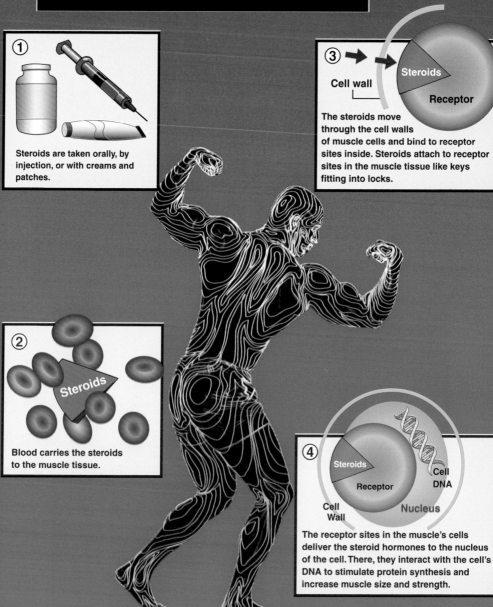

① Steroids are taken orally, by injection, or with creams and patches.

③ Cell wall • Steroids • Receptor

The steroids move through the cell walls of muscle cells and bind to receptor sites inside. Steroids attach to receptor sites in the muscle tissue like keys fitting into locks.

② Steroids

Blood carries the steroids to the muscle tissue.

④ Steroids • Receptor • Cell DNA • Cell Wall • Nucleus

The receptor sites in the muscle's cells deliver the steroid hormones to the nucleus of the cell. There, they interact with the cell's DNA to stimulate protein synthesis and increase muscle size and strength.

the cell to produce more protein. "They work very much like a lock and key to cause muscles to increase the amount of protein they make,"[21] explains Thomas D. Fahey of California State University, Chico.

Recent research by Bhasin and his associates has led to another hypothesis. The researchers noted that anabolic steroids seem to decrease fat mass along with increasing muscle mass. After a series of experiments, they concluded that anabolic steroids affect several cell types, including stem cells, which have the potential to become many different kinds of cells. When testosterone binds to receptors on these cells, it may

This computer image shows the chemical components of testosterone, a naturally-occurring steroid in the human body.

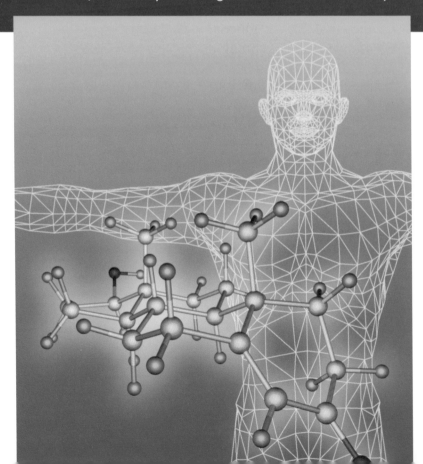

signal them to form muscle precursor cells, which then fuse together to increase the size of existing muscle fiber. According to Bhasin, "Although the data are still emerging, our initial findings suggest that androgens promote stem cells to differentiate in a way that increases formation of muscle cells and inhibits formation of fat cells. So you get more muscle and less fat."[22]

Another possible effect of anabolic steroids is interference with a group of naturally-produced steroids called glucocorticoids. Glucocorticoids are catabolic, meaning they break down muscle. The body secretes them during exercise or other stress to burn protein for fuel and to fight inflammation. Fahey explains, "When you lift weights, you have two processes that are initiated. You're going to have a muscle-building process and a muscle-breakdown process."[23] Some researchers think that anabolic steroids bind to receptors for glucocorticoids. The glucocorticoids are blocked from their receptors and from sending the signal to break down muscle. This would lead to a quicker recovery time between workouts and would explain why most athletes on anabolic steroids claim that they can work out more frequently and intensely.

Anabolic steroids could also have an indirect effect on muscles by increasing aggression so that athletes train harder. Although increased aggression has been difficult to demonstrate in studies, athletes commonly report this side effect.

The effects of anabolic steroids on body composition are not permanent. When users stop taking the drugs, they lose their steroid-induced muscle gains. One factor overlooked by many users is that the testosterone they take into their bodies suppresses their natural production. "When they stop taking testosterone, their levels are actually lower than where they started, and it takes a long time for their own body to recover testosterone production,"[24] Bhasin points out. These abnormally low testosterone levels could allow faster loss of muscle gains and could cause a hormonal depression. These factors sometimes lead to psychological dependence on the drugs.

Lingering Distrust

A 2004 study by researchers at Harvard Medical School indicates that the medical community has not regained its credibility with athletes who use anabolic steroids. Researchers interviewed eighty weight lifters, forty-three of whom were anabolic steroid users and thirty-seven of whom were nonusers, and asked them to rate their trust in physicians' knowledge of various health-related issues. Both users and nonusers gave doctors similar high ratings in areas of health and disease, cigarette smoking, and use of alcohol and street drugs. When it came to anabolic steroids, however, users rated doctors' knowledge much lower than nonusers did.

The authors believed the lack of trust in physicians stemmed from the medical community's long-term denial that anabolic steroids build muscle and from the perception that physicians do not understand the "bodybuilding lifestyle." They concluded, "These 'attitude problems' among AAS (anabolic-androgenic steroid) users may have serious public-health consequences, because they compromise the ability of professionals to study, educate, or treat these individuals."

Identifying Users

Because anabolic steroids allow users to develop a degree of muscularity not possible without drugs, the trained eye can identify users by their appearance. After studying hundreds of subjects, both users and nonusers, Harrison G. Pope Jr. of McLean Hospital and his colleagues believe they have identified the upper limit of muscularity possible for a nonuser and that men who exceed this limit have almost certainly used anabolic steroids. The researchers calculate muscularity with a formula that uses the person's height, weight, and body-fat percentage.

Another sign of anabolic steroid use is disproportionate upper body mass. Since anabolic steroids have the greatest effect in the upper body, users' shoulders, necks, and chest muscles may look unnaturally large compared with other areas of the body.

Anabolic Effects Applied to Medicine

Despite the long-standing debate over the anabolic effects of these drugs, they have been used for decades to treat patients suffering from wasting conditions. Doctors prescribe anabolic steroids to promote healing in burn or trauma victims and to strengthen weak patients before and after surgery or after radiation therapy. Patients treated with anabolic steroids have gained muscle mass and strength and have reported improved appetite and sense of well-being.

The confirmation during the 1980s and 1990s that anabolic steroids build muscle has led to renewed interest in developing versions more appropriate for use in patients afflicted with wasting diseases, such as AIDS or cancer, and in elderly people. Bhasin says, "If we can increase their muscle mass and strength and increase their mobility, it can make all the difference between being completely dependent or bedridden and being independent. And that can make a huge difference in both quality of life and the cost of caring for these individuals."[25] Since evidence indicates that anabolic steroids can adversely affect the heart and prostate, researchers are trying to develop versions with anabolic properties but without these adverse effects.

Useful Effects on Hormone and Sperm Levels

The earliest medical use for synthetic anabolic steroids was treatment of hypogonadism, a condition in which the body does not produce enough testosterone. Physicians continue to prescribe anabolic steroids for this purpose. As replacement therapy, these drugs raise testosterone levels to normal and allow patients to develop or maintain male sexual characteristics and normal muscle size.

Studies conducted in the 1990s have led to increased use of anabolic steroids as replacement therapy in healthy older men, whose bodies produce less testosterone because of age. At the other end of the spectrum, boys aged fifteen or older who have not entered puberty are treated with anabolic steroids for six months. The drugs trigger puberty to begin, after which the boys' bodies begin producing normal amounts of testosterone.

The effect of anabolic steroids on sperm levels has resulted in other medical applications. Higher-than-normal levels of testosterone in the male body lead to suppression of sperm production, and these drugs have been successfully tested as a male contraceptive. The effect is reversible when use is discontinued. On the other hand, the drugs can help restore fertility in men with low sperm counts. These men are given high doses of anabolic steroids to suppress their sperm production for several months. When they stop taking the drugs, a rebound effect often causes their natural sperm production to increase to levels higher than before.

Other Medical Applications

Anabolic steroids have limited medical applications in women. Beginning in the 1940s, these drugs were given to women with advanced estrogen-related breast cancers so that they could counteract the estrogen and shrink the tumors. Other drugs without the masculinizing side effects are now used for this purpose. Anabolic steroids with weaker androgenic effects are sometimes used to treat endometriosis, a condition in which tissue lining the uterus grows in other parts of the body and can cause pain, bleeding, and infertility. Anabolic steroids help control this condition by reducing levels of female hormones.

In both men and women with hereditary angioedema, a disorder in which sufferers experience attacks of swelling in the face, limbs, hands, feet, intestines, or airway, anabolic steroids help prevent such attacks. Hereditary angioedema can be life-threatening since the airway may swell shut. Anabolic steroids are also prescribed to treat rare forms of anemia, although newer drugs are more commonly used for this purpose.

An early medical application for anabolic steroids was treatment of depression, but by the 1950s they were largely replaced with other drugs and electroconvulsive (electroshock) therapy. Recent studies have renewed interest in psychiatric use by demonstrating that anabolic steroids may be an effective tool for treating depression in men who do not respond to conventional antidepressants and in men infected with HIV.

Anabolic steroids have some of the same medical applications for animals as for humans. Veterinarians prescribe anabolic steroids to improve appetite and strength in older animals and in animals that have been weakened by surgery or illness. Some types are given to cattle to increase their weight gain. As in humans, the drugs are often used in racehorses for performance enhancement. Many of the anabolic steroids humans purchase on the black market were produced for veterinary use.

In addition to improved athletic ability in humans, the drugs can be used to enhance the performance of racehorses and other animals.

Corticosteroids

Because of the public attention anabolic steroids receive, many people automatically think of them when they hear the term *steroids*. Anabolic steroids are only one group of the compounds known as steroids. Other groups of steroids, including glucocorticoids and female hormones, are not anabolic. These also have synthetic counterparts that physicians prescribe for medical problems.

The most commonly prescribed steroids are corticosteroids, such as cortisone and prednisone. These are synthetic versions of glucocorticoids, which naturally are produced by the adrenal glands. Rather than build muscle, these catabolic steroids break down tissue and fight inflammation.

Doctors discovered the anti-inflammatory effect of cortisone in 1948, when they used it to treat a twenty-nine-year-old woman who was immobilized with severe rheumatoid arthritis. After two cortisone injections, her pain and swelling decreased and she was able to walk. Other arthritis patients treated with the new drug likewise experienced remarkable results. Three researchers whose work led to this medical breakthrough were awarded the Nobel Prize for physiology and medicine in 1950.

Because of cortisone's early success, many viewed it as a miracle drug. Over time, however, side effects became evident in patients who took high doses for extended periods. Corticosteroids increase the risk of high blood pressure by making the body retain water and salt. Because they cause calcium loss from bones, these drugs put older adults at increased risk for osteoporosis. They also increase blood sugar, making it difficult for diabetics to control their disease. Patients who contract chicken pox or measles may find that corticosteroid use makes the infection more serious. In children, long-term use may slow growth, but it is unknown whether this affects final adult height.

The medical benefits of corticosteroid treatment led doctors to develop strategies for reducing the side effects. Some patients

Besides alarming patients who misunderstand what their doctors have prescribed, steroid confusion can trigger false positives in surveys. Some who respond that they have used anabolic steroids may in fact have used corticosteroids, such as cortisone. On the other hand, some who have used anabolic steroids may decline to say so, thus lowering the number of positive responses.

In 2005, newspapers reported that 5 percent of high school girls and 7 percent of middle school girls admitted having tried anabolic steroids. Some researchers believed these percentages were unrealistic and that some of the girls, especially those in the younger group, had confused anabolic steroids with corticosteroids they had taken for asthma or poison ivy.

In a few cases, bodybuilders who thought they were taking anabolic steroids were actually taking corticosteroids or female hormones. Besides having no muscle-building properties, these other groups of steroids can

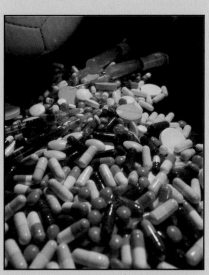

cause unwelcome side effects in those who have no medical need for them. For example, estrogen can cause gynecomastia (abnormal enlargement of breast tissue) in male users.

Although anabolic steroids are primarily used as performance enhancers, the drugs also have legitimate medical uses.

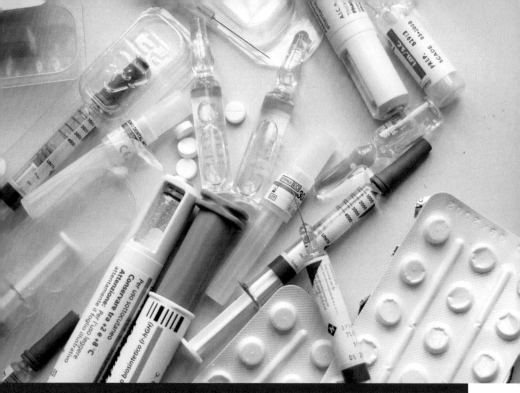

Pictured here is a wide variety of anabolic steroids, in both pill and liquid form, with syringes used to inject the liquid variety.

can take lower doses for shorter periods of time. Exercise and diet help counteract weight gain and the risk of osteoporosis in patients who must take the drugs for extended periods.

Patient fear of corticosteroid side effects is only one factor that led to the coining of the term *steroidophobia*. Another is the amount of media attention given to the negative effects of anabolic steroids. Many patients confuse the two types of steroids and resist the idea of any steroid treatment. David B. Allen of the University of Wisconsin Children's Hospital says, "We have heard about the perception that steroids are bad. And our patients definitely have this perception. When we talk about using these medications for their children, they don't know that we're not talking about anabolic steroids, or what they're reading about on the grocery store shelf. It's quite confusing."[26] He recommends that health care professionals take time to educate their patients about the difference between anabolic steroids and corticosteroids.

Dozens of corticosteroids are available for medical use today. Besides arthritis inflammation, the drugs are used to treat such problems as asthma, allergies, lupus, and muscle strains and to prevent rejection of transplanted organs. Corticosteroids are prescribed as replacement therapy for patients with Addison's disease, a rare but life-threatening disease in which the adrenal glands do not produce enough glucocorticoids.

Female Hormones

Another group of steroids includes the female hormones estrogen and progesterone. The female body's natural production of estrogen is reduced at menopause, which leads to symptoms such as hot flashes, sweating, and vaginal discomfort. Doctors prescribe synthetic estrogen as replacement therapy to alleviate these symptoms and to prevent osteoporosis. The side effects of taking estrogen may include increased risk of breast cancer, heart attack, stroke, and blood clots. Progestin (a synthetic form of progesterone) is combined with estrogen in hormone replacement therapy to decrease the risk of uterine cancer.

Doctors also prescribe combinations of estrogen and progestin in the form of oral contraceptives. On its own, progestin can also be used as a contraceptive, to regulate menstrual cycles, or to help a woman become pregnant and maintain the pregnancy when her body does not produce enough of this hormone. Progestin helps increase appetite and weight gain in cancer or AIDS patients and helps stop tumor growth in patients with breast, kidney, or uterine cancer. Estrogen also helps fight certain types of cancer in both men and women.

Doctors prescribe female hormones, corticosteroids, and, in rare cases, anabolic steroids when they believe the medical benefits outweigh the danger from side effects. Most anabolic steroid users, however, take these drugs illegally for performance enhancement or appearance, with no medical justification for the risk. That risk includes a wide range of side effects, some known, others suspected. Anabolic steroids have a dark side that cannot be ignored.

Chapter 3

Success with a Price

A long list of side effects is attributed to anabolic steroids, but this list is accompanied by much debate. While some side effects are well documented, much remains unknown about the long-term health hazards. Some researchers believe that the media has contributed to the confusion by publishing sensational reports that exaggerate the risks. Meanwhile, many users pay a high price for ignoring those risks.

The Effects on Female Users

The effects of anabolic steroids on physical appearance are well known. As the primary male hormone, testosterone is responsible for development of secondary male sexual characteristics. The increase in testosterone that males experience at puberty accounts for many of the physical differences between males and females. Females who take anabolic steroids to build muscle also experience the other masculinizing effects of these drugs, including a deepened voice, growth of facial and body hair, loss of scalp hair, an enlarged clitoris, and an increase in libido. These effects may be irreversible.

Although the masculinizing effects on females were evident when anabolic steroids were first used in medicine in the 1930s, that did not stop female athletes from later using these drugs for performance enhancement. Since the adult female body normally produces only 0.3 milligrams of testosterone a day, compared with 7 milligrams a day produced by the adult male body, anabolic steroid use can make a marked difference in muscle size and strength for female users. For this reason, the government-sponsored sports-doping program in the German Democratic Republic (GDR) emphasized administering anabolic steroids to women and adolescent girls.

After the fall of the GDR in 1990, more than 150 formerly classified government documents confirmed the existence of the doping program and revealed its extent. Beginning in 1966 thousands of athletes were given anabolic steroids each year. The age at which steroid administration began depended on the sport, but female swimmers aged fourteen or

POSSIBLE CONSEQUENCES OF STEROID USE

Below is a listing of the various hormonal side effects associated with steroid use. These consequences have been grouped according to gender.

In males

▶ breast enlargement

▶ infertility

▶ shrinking of the testicles

▶ enlargement of the prostate gland, which can lead to difficulty or pain when urinating

▶ male-pattern baldness

▶ testosterone production stopped

In females

▶ irreversible loss of scalp hair

▶ irreversible lowering of the voice

▶ menstrual irregularities

▶ decreased breast size

▶ irreversible and excessive hair growth on body and face

▶ enlarged clitoris

▶ sex drive increased

▶ fetal damage in pregnant women

Despite the masculinizing side effects of anabolic steroids, surveys conducted during the 1990s showed that use of these drugs was growing faster among young women than among any other group. Besides athletes whose motive is performance enhancement, an increasing number of young women take anabolic steroids in an effort to attain a lean, muscular look.

Some female users may have a distorted body image, so that they do not recognize the masculinizing changes. Others are willing to do whatever it takes to excel at their sport.

In some cases, anabolic steroid abuse may be a reaction to the trauma of sexual assault. In a study of female weight lifters that included ten rape victims, researchers Amanda J. Gruber and Harrison G. Pope Jr. found that nine of these women increased their bodybuilding activities after the attack and seven began using anabolic steroids or another muscle-building drug. They wanted to increase their muscle strength and size in order to protect themselves and to discourage future attacks. One of these anabolic steroid users stated that she wanted to look more masculine so that men would find her less attractive.

younger and fourteen- to fifteen-year-old males and females in some other sports were treated with male hormones, without the knowledge of their parents. The athletes, physicians, and coaches involved were sworn to secrecy. In some cases, athletes were given experimental drugs that had not been approved for use in humans. The users included many world-record holders and Olympic medalists.

The documents reported severe masculinizing effects in female users. Many of the doctors involved stated that it was unethical to administer male hormones to females, but they followed the government's instructions. In 1977 Manfred Höppner reported to the government, "In numerous women the prevailing administration of anabolic hormones has resulted in irreversible damages, in particular in the swimming events, for example signs of virilization such as an increased growth of bodily hair (hirsutism), voice changes and disturbances in libido."[27] He related the case of a two-time gold medal winner whose voice had deepened to the point that she could no longer perform her work as an interpreter.

Female athletes who were troubled by the masculinizing side effects were not allowed to stop taking the drugs. Höppner reported on his examination of a teenage sprinter who was a world-record holder: "The legs including the inner parts of the thighs are strongly hirsute and the pubic hair extends already to the navel. She is forced to shave."[28] The sprinter had been given anabolic steroids since age fifteen by her coach, who told her they were vitamin tablets. When she recognized from the side effects that she was taking anabolic steroids, she decided to give up her sprinting career but was told she would be expelled from school and lose all support. Although Höppner arranged permission for her to graduate, this was an exception.

Many female athletes in the program experienced gynecological problems, such as ovarian cysts. Because doctors believed that anabolic steroid use by the mother could cause birth defects in early pregnancy, female athletes were given oral contraceptive pills. If an athlete became pregnant, an abortion was ordered.

Testosterone Overload

While anabolic steroids masculinize women, they have the ironic effect of causing feminizing changes in men. A male body overloaded with testosterone converts some of the excess testosterone into the female hormone estrogen. As a result, male steroid users may develop gynecomastia, an abnormal enlargement of breast tissue. In mild cases, the effect may disappear once anabolic steroid use is discontinued, but severe cases require surgery for correction. In the GDR, twelve weight lifters underwent surgery to remove the excess breast tissue.

When the male body contains abnormally high testosterone levels, the pituitary gland seeks to correct the imbalance by shutting down the body's natural testosterone production. The testes shrink, and sperm production is reduced. Depending on the type and dosage of the anabolic steroid, users may become infertile while taking the drugs and for up to six months after stopping. Some researchers believe that high doses taken over a long period could cause permanent infertility, but this has not been proven.

Another hormonal side effect, acne, results because anabolic steroids increase oil gland secretions in the skin. This is common in both male and female users and may be severe. Both genders may also experience loss of scalp hair. In men, male-pattern baldness accelerates, and women experience thinning all over the scalp.

Users try to minimize side effects by taking anabolic steroids in cycles of from four to twenty weeks, although some users never go off the drugs. They may also take drugs such as human choriotic gonadotropin to prevent the testes from shrinking, anti-acne medications, and anti-estrogens.

Musculoskeletal Risks

Anabolic steroid use carries added risks for adolescents. Puberty begins with a large increase in testosterone production for males and a slight increase for females. Anabolic steroid use speeds up adolescent growth so that the epiphyses, or growth plates at the ends of the long bones, fuse together earlier than they normally would. The result is permanently lost growth. Charles E. Yesalis of Penn State University explains the effect: "If God intended you to be six-two and you start taking steroids when you're five-four, you might be a very muscular five-four, but you're not going to be as tall as you would have been."[29]

Some believe that because anabolic steroids cause muscles to grow at an abnormal rate, the tendons connecting these muscles to the bones are not strong enough to support the extra bulk and may rupture more easily. Animal studies suggest that anabolic steroids may also affect the elasticity of tendons, which would lead to more injuries. Since many athletes experience these types of injuries regardless of whether they use anabolic steroids, it is difficult to prove the link.

Steroid abuse among adolescents can result in serious health problems, as a result of the increased levels of testosterone in the body.

As an indirect side effect, the extra mass may pose a threat of injury to other players. Indianapolis Colts linebacker Johnnie Cooks expressed his frustration in 1986: "Steroids are the worst problem in the NFL. I just want to play foot-

East German Athletes Seek Justice

Decades after the fall of the GDR, hundreds of former East German athletes suffer from serious health problems, including heart and liver disease and cancer, which they attribute to the anabolic steroids administered to them under the sports-doping program. Besides enduring masculinizing effects, some female athletes experience recurring ovarian cysts and have had miscarriages or have given birth to children with club feet.

In a series of criminal trials that ended in the year 2000, Dr. Manfred Höppner and other East German officials were convicted of causing bodily harm to athletes. They received only suspended jail sentences and fines, which left many former athletes feeling that justice had not been served.

In 2005, 160 former East German athletes filed a class-action lawsuit against Jenapharm, a pharmaceutical company that produced the anabolic steroids used in the doping program. According to Michael Lehner, the lawyer representing the former athletes, "When somebody suffers from liver damage for the rest of his life, when a woman has disabled children or is always mistaken for a man, no money and no amends can compensate for that." Jenapharm's chief executive said that the company had no choice but to cooperate with the government and that it could not be held responsible for misuse of its products.

ball with the body the Lord gave me. Some of these guys we play are nothing but muscle. When you get hit by them, something has to go."[30]

Case Reports vs. Scientific Studies

A lack of scientific data means that much is still unknown about the long-term health hazards of anabolic steroid abuse. Numerous case reports exist of users who experienced heart and liver disease and prostate problems. Case reports are considered unreliable because researchers have no way of knowing how other factors, such as use of alcohol or other drugs, diet, and heredity, affected users' risks of developing these problems. In order to determine the role anabolic steroids play, researchers need evidence from scientific studies that control other factors and that compare subjects given anabolic steroids with subjects given a placebo. No long-term, placebo-controlled studies have been conducted on athletes taking anabolic steroids.

Prostate and Liver Effects

One of the earliest effects noted in male athletes using anabolic steroids was enlargement of the prostate gland. Although studies show that anabolic steroids can produce prostate cancer in rats, it has not been proven that these drugs cause the disease in humans. If a man with prostate cancer takes anabolic steroids, his condition will worsen since this type of cancer is androgen sensitive. As Yesalis explains, "If you have it, it would be like throwing gasoline on a fire."[31]

Case reports and evidence from patients treated with some types of oral anabolic steroids show toxic effects on the liver, which removes anabolic steroids from the body. Some patients suffering from jaundice, a condition in which the skin and whites of the eyes turn yellow due to blocked bile flow, found their condition worsened, and other patients developed jaundice. The jaundice usually disappears a few weeks after patients stop using the drugs.

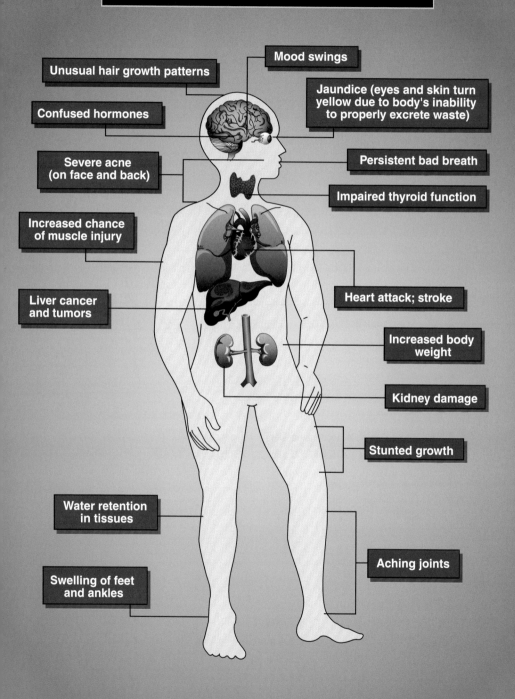

POSSIBLE PHYSICAL EFFECTS OF STEROIDS

Mood swings

Unusual hair growth patterns

Jaundice (eyes and skin turn yellow due to body's inability to properly excrete waste)

Confused hormones

Severe acne (on face and back)

Persistent bad breath

Impaired thyroid function

Increased chance of muscle injury

Liver cancer and tumors

Heart attack; stroke

Increased body weight

Kidney damage

Stunted growth

Water retention in tissues

Aching joints

Swelling of feet and ankles

Other liver problems can be life-threatening. These types of anabolic steroids have been implicated in peliosis hepatis, a condition in which blood-filled cysts form in the liver. If the cysts rupture, patients can die, and they may not be aware of their disease until it is too late. Although peliosis hepatis is rare, more than seventy cases were reported among anabolic steroid users from 1952 to 1990.

These drugs also increase the risk of liver tumors. Most of these tumors are benign, but they are life-threatening because they can rupture and cause severe internal bleeding and death. As with peliosis hepatis, patients with liver tumors may not show symptoms until a rupture occurs.

Höppner reported to the GDR government that several male and female athletes in the sports-doping program had developed severe liver problems. He believed that in some male athletes the problem resulted from the combination of anabolic steroid use and alcohol consumption and that in female athletes the combination of anabolic steroids and oral contraceptives increased the damage.

Heart Disease

Although no controlled study exists to prove that anabolic steroids increase the risk of heart disease, several factors lead researchers to believe that they may. Anabolic steroid use decreases the level of high-density lipoprotein cholesterol (HDLC), which is commonly called the "good cholesterol." Thomas D. Fahey of California State University, Chico, explains: "HDLC is considered a positive risk factor of heart disease, meaning that it actually prevents heart disease. So if you have low levels of [HDLC], in theory this should increase your risk of heart attack."[32]

Some types of steroids have been shown to cause glucose intolerance, a condition in which blood sugar levels are higher than normal but not high enough to merit a diagnosis of diabetes. Glucose intolerance also increases the risk of heart disease. Case reports from athletes using anabolic steroids and

patients treated with these drugs for medical problems suggest that high doses of anabolic steroids may cause thrombotic stroke, the type of stroke that occurs when a blood clot develops in an artery and cuts off the flow of blood to the brain. Additionally, several athletes using anabolic steroids have developed dilated cardiomyopathy, a condition in which the heart becomes enlarged and does not pump efficiently. It is difficult for researchers to determine whether these cases were caused by anabolic steroids, other risk factors, or a combination.

One well-publicized case report illustrates the confusion. In 1985 NFL offensive lineman Steve Courson became the first NFL player to publicly admit anabolic steroid use. When he later developed cardiomyopathy, some members of the sports media blamed the disease on steroids. Because other risk factors, including alcohol abuse, were involved, doctors diagnosed the disease as idiopathic, or of unknown cause. Courson says, "I believe that since the drugs, combined with training and diet, contributed to my body size, [they] together with stress and alcohol added more to an already dangerous mix."[33]

A Famous Case

Another former NFL player, Lyle Alzado, was outspoken in his belief that performance-enhancing drugs caused his inoperable brain cancer. Alzado took anabolic steroids without stopping from 1969 until he was diagnosed with the disease in 1991. He also began taking human growth hormone in 1990. No other case is known of an anabolic steroid user developing this disease. Alzado once said, "I know there's no written, documented proof that steroids and human growth hormone caused this cancer. But it's one of the reasons you have to look at. You have to. And I think that there are a lot of athletes in danger."[34] He died from the disease in 1992 at age forty-three.

One of Alzado's doctors, Robert Huizenga, acknowledged that much is unknown about the long-term effects of anabolic steroids. Because of the lack of scientific studies,

Former NFL star Lyle Alzado was convinced that steroid abuse over the course of more than two decades caused his terminal brain cancer.

and because of estimates that a million Americans may be using anabolic steroids, Huizenga concluded, "I think we have a real time bomb on our hands."[35]

Related Threats

Anabolic steroid abuse also carries indirect hazards. Users who inject these drugs run the risk of contracting AIDS, hepatitis, or other infections from contaminated needles. Steroids produced in underground laboratories and sold on the black market may be contaminated or may contain ingredients not listed on the package. In some cases, these counterfeit drugs contain no anabolic steroid.

Studies of men admitted to substance abuse treatment have suggested that anabolic steroid use may lead to abuse of opioids, such as heroin. Some of the anabolic steroid users in these studies learned about opioids from other anabolic

steroid users and bought them from the dealer who had previously sold them anabolic steroids.

Detecting Aggression

As with the physical effects, the psychological effects of anabolic steroids have been steeped in debate. Many users report increased aggression that allows them to train harder.
In some cases, the aggression leads to violent, out-of-control
behavior that has been dubbed *'roid rage*. Although animal
studies show increased aggression from anabolic steroid use,
studies on humans have yielded mixed results. In some studies that used small doses, subjects reported no increase in
aggression. This led some researchers to suggest that the
connection between anabolic steroids and aggressive behavior was a myth.

In four newer studies, researchers gave subjects doses of
five hundred milligrams per week or higher. In three of those
studies, a minority of subjects experienced increased aggression. Since these studies were conducted under double-blind
conditions, in which study subjects and the researchers in
contact with them did not know who was getting the anabolic steroid and who was getting a placebo, this helped rule
out the possibility that the increased aggression resulted from
the power of suggestion.

These study results are in line with observations made on
athletes in the field, which indicate that psychological effects
are rare with doses under three hundred milligrams per
week. Some users who take between three hundred and one
thousand milligrams per week experience symptoms such as
irritability, recklessness, euphoria, decreased need for sleep,
grandiose beliefs, and violent behavior. These symptoms become more common at doses above one thousand milligrams per week.

Scientists are limited in their ability to study this dosage
effect. "Nobody can ethically do a study where we inten-
tionally give people doses way above 1000 mg a week—unless

they have consented to stay on in an inpatient ward—because it would be too dangerous," explains Harrison G. Pope Jr. of McLean Hospital. "As a result, it is impossible to replicate in the laboratory under double-blind conditions the very high doses that are used by many actual illicit steroid users in the field."[36] Because of this, the percentage of actual users affected could be much higher than the percentage affected in the laboratory.

Other contributing factors may be the type of anabolic steroid, the length of time it is used, and whether it is used in combination with other drugs. Since these factors vary considerably, it is difficult to draw comparisons between users. Thomas W. Storer of the University of California, Los Angeles (UCLA), offers an example:

Researchers continue to debate whether or not there is a link between long-term steroid use and increased aggression.

While many physicians believe high doses of steroids are dangerous to the user, the lasting effects of the drug remain unknown.

If an older man with below-normal testosterone takes a therapeutic dose to bring his testosterone back up to the normal range, and he takes it for a relatively short period of time, he is less likely to exhibit any of these untoward behavior changes. However, a person with normal testosterone, who takes a high dose for performance enhancement or aesthetics and is taking it for a long period of time, may be providing a more substantial trigger. And the same is probably true with other side effects.[37]

Although most researchers now agree that anabolic steroids can increase aggression, a 1994 study indicates that some users who expect to feel more aggressive may be influenced by the power of suggestion. Researchers found that participants who were given a placebo they believed to be an anabolic steroid showed increased aggression. The researchers concluded that widespread belief in the connection between anabolic steroids and aggression could affect users' behavior. According to the researchers, "It may, in fact, work as an excuse for aggression."[38]

On the other hand, Shalender Bhasin of UCLA has suggested that increased aggression might sometimes go undetected in studies because humans recognize the need to exercise self-control:

> In humans it's been very difficult to study, and part of it is that many of the instruments we use to detect aggression, angry behaviors, et cetera, are limited in that overt expression of anger and aggression is constrained by the social stigma associated with these behaviors. We don't approve of these behaviors, so people—at least people with any degree of education—will restrain these behaviors.[39]

From One Extreme to the Other

No one knows why only a minority of users become violently aggressive. According to Pope, "It does not appear to be associated with your prior personality, your family history, or your own psychiatric history."[40] In cases of anabolic steroid users charged with robbery, rape, murder, and attempted murder, some had no previous history of violence or mood disorders. Danger lies in the fact that users cannot predict whether they will be affected.

Some accused criminals have used 'roid rage as a defense in court. In the first such case, Michael David Williams, a twenty-six-year-old bodybuilder, burglarized six homes and set three of them on fire in June 1985. His attorney argued that Williams's heavy anabolic steroid use was to blame. The judge concluded that Williams was "suffering from an organic personality syndrome caused by the toxic levels of anabolic steroids taken to enhance his ability to win the body-building contests, and . . . this disorder substantially impaired his ability to appreciate the criminality of his acts."[41] The judge sentenced Williams to outpatient psychological counseling.

Reports indicate that increased aggression goes away when anabolic steroid use is stopped, but at this point another psychological effect may surface. Some users seem to become dependent on the drugs and become depressed when they try to stop. Depression can result from losing steroid-induced muscle gains, but it may also have a hormonal link. The bodies of heavy users stop producing testosterone naturally in response to the abnormally high levels present. When they stop using the drugs, it may take weeks for their bodies to begin producing testosterone again.

Playing with Fire

More research is needed to answer all the questions about the physical and psychological effects of anabolic steroids. But Yesalis warns that it would be a mistake for users to close their eyes to the possible dangers. After acknowledging that doctors prescribe anabolic steroids for certain medical problems, he says, "Anabolic steroids, if used judiciously, under a physician's supervision, can they be used fairly safely? Yeah. Do I believe you can hurt yourself with them if you take them in high doses for long periods of time? These things are too powerful to think you can fool Mother Nature."[42]

Besides concerns over health effects, anabolic steroid abuse has raised issues over fairness in sports. Researchers have taken on the challenge of developing testing methods to keep anabolic steroids out of athletic competition.

Chapter 4

A Game of Cat and Mouse

During the 1960s scientists made great progress in the drug-testing field. Also during that decade, several athletes died during competition from the use of amphetamines. Concern over the safety of athletes, coupled with the desire to ensure fair competition, moved the International Olympic Committee (IOC) to outlaw doping and set up testing labs. In the decades that followed, other sporting organizations implemented drug-testing policies, although the strictness of these policies varies.

Scientists work continually to develop new and more sensitive testing methods that detect a larger array of banned substances. At the same time, athletes and underground chemists develop methods to get around the tests, in a seemingly never-ending cycle.

The Beginnings of Systematic Drug Testing

In 1967 the IOC drafted rules against doping, which it defined as the "use of substances or techniques in any form or quantity alien or unnatural to the body with the exclusive aim of obtaining an artificial or unfair increase of performance in

IOC president Jacques Rogge participates in a press conference addressing the issue of drug testing during the 2004 Olympic Games.

competition."[43] Random drug testing began at the 1968 Olympic Winter Games. At that time, no test existed to detect anabolic steroids, so they were not included in the process.

In 1973 researchers at the University of London reported that they had developed the first tests capable of detecting anabolic steroids. With radioimmunoassay (RIA) screening, urine was tested against antibodies that researchers had developed to react with anabolic steroids. These antibodies also react with molecules that are similar to anabolic steroids, so any positive results from RIA had to be confirmed with a second, more specific test, gas chromatography/mass spectrometry (GC/MS).

In GC/MS, the urine sample is first processed to purify and concentrate the substances it contains. The resulting extract is placed in the gas chromatograph, where it is vaporized and passed through a long glass column. Since different substances pass through at different rates, the amount of time a substance spends in the column helps identify it. The substance then enters the mass spectrometer, where a beam of electrons breaks apart the substance's molecules. The mass spectrometer separates the fragments and measures their masses. Scientists identify the substance by matching its results from the gas chromatograph and the mass spectrometer with those of a known substance.

The IOC adopted both tests, using RIA to analyze urine samples and GC/MS to confirm positive results. Since the 1984 Olympic Games, GC/MS has been used for both steps because of its greater specificity. In recent years some drug-testing labs have added liquid chromatography/mass spectrometry (LC/MS), in which the sample does not need to be vaporized.

The new tests were introduced at competitions in 1974 and 1975 and were put into Olympic use at the 1976 Montreal Games. At those Olympics, 275 samples were tested for anabolic steroids, with 8 positive results.

Targeting Testosterone

Positive tests were few from 1976 to 1980, but not necessarily because few athletes were using anabolic steroids. When a test was announced, some athletes claimed sudden illnesses or injuries and withdrew from competition to avoid being tested. Unlike performance-enhancing drugs such as amphetamines, which must be taken at the time of competition to be effective, anabolic steroids are used during training. Athletes who stopped using these drugs far enough in advance could avoid detection. Others found a way around the tests by switching from modified anabolic steroids to testosterone. Synthetic testosterone has the same chemical structure as testosterone produced by the body, so GC/MS could not identify it as a foreign substance.

Manfred Donike, head of the IOC lab in Cologne, West Germany, addressed the problem by developing a test to detect abnormally high testosterone levels. This test, called the T/E ratio, compares the amount of testosterone in the body with the amount of the hormone epitestosterone. Most adult men have a T/E ratio of 1:1, but natural testosterone levels vary, with an estimated chance of one in three thousand that a drug-free man could have a T/E ratio as high as 6:1. To avoid false positives, Donike set the limit at 6:1, meaning that the athlete's body could contain six times as much testosterone as epitestosterone. A level higher than that was considered proof that the athlete was taking testosterone from the outside.

Donike put the new test to the proof at the 1980 Moscow Olympics, where he unofficially measured the T/E ratio of urine samples. The tests officially in use detected no anabolic steroids in athletes' urine, but Donike found that 20 percent of the athletes, including sixteen gold medalists, had T/E ratios higher than 6:1. This indicated that many athletes had switched from modified anabolic steroids to testosterone. Al-

President of the U.S. Olympic Committee William E. Simon (left) had no sympathy for athletes upset by drug tests administered at the 1983 Pan American games.

though these athletes were not sanctioned, the new test had revealed the magnitude of the problem, and the IOC adopted it for official use.

When Donike used the new test officially for the first time at the 1983 Pan American Games in Caracas, Venezuela, many athletes were caught off guard. Nineteen athletes tested positive for anabolic steroids, and twelve were stripped of medals. When athletes saw how sensitive the testing was, some withdrew from competition. Others competed far below their abilities since winning athletes were automatically tested and the others were tested at random. When some athletes complained that they had not been warned about the strictness of the testing procedures, U.S. Olympic Committee (USOC) president William E. Simon responded, "The fact is, they broke the law, and the fact is, they knew what the law was, and the fact is that they knew what the penalty was. And them's the rules, so don't complain if you get caught. No sympathy here, thank you."[44]

The T/E ratio did not solve the problem completely. Because most athletes have a natural T/E ratio much lower than 6:1, they could take smaller amounts of testosterone and stay below the legal limit. Since the female body responds quickly to testosterone, female athletes could experience great gains by taking small amounts. For women, this was a double-edged sword. To avoid detection, some switched from versions of anabolic steroids that have weaker androgenic effects to pure testosterone, with its potential for severe masculinization. Other athletes, both male and female, began using synthetic human growth hormone, which was undetectable in urine but came with its own list of severe side effects.

Labs That Help, Labs That Hinder

In 1980 the IOC wrote strict requirements for its drug-testing labs. Ironically, the East German government secretly used the IOC-accredited lab in that country to help its athletes circumvent drug tests. This lab tested athletes' urine to determine

how long it took anabolic steroids to clear their bodies. Athletes switched to testosterone before competition. When the T/E ratio was put in use, the East German lab tested its athletes' urine to make sure they were within the legal limit before they departed for competition. If an athlete tested positive, he or she did not compete. Athletes were also given epitestosterone in addition to testosterone to balance out their T/E ratio. Despite widespread anabolic steroid use among East German athletes, none tested positive after 1977.

In 1988 the IOC sought to prevent such abuses by writing a code of ethics forbidding its labs from doing drug testing for individuals. Nonetheless, some athletes use the services of commercial labs to monitor their T/E ratios or to determine how far in advance of competition they must discontinue anabolic steroid use to test clean.

Addressing Thorny Problems

The doping problem drew worldwide attention in 1988, when Canadian sprinter Ben Johnson tested positive for anabolic steroids and was stripped of his gold medal after a world-record win in the one-hundred-meter sprint. At that time, all testing was done at competitions. Although Johnson admitted that he had been using anabolic steroids for a long time, he had previously passed nineteen drug tests. This incident highlighted the need for out-of-competition testing. "It was a real wake-up call to sport,"[45] says Don H. Catlin, head of the Olympic Lab at the University of California, Los Angeles (UCLA).

Some sporting federations introduced out-of-competition testing, but it was limited by the high cost of sending testers out to find the athletes and collect their urine. In 1995 Ralph Hale, USOC vice president, lamented, "Our anti-doping campaign, I'm afraid, has been a failure to this point. Many countries have lost confidence in our anti-doping effort. I'm not sure we're doing the right job."[46] USOC medical experts called for an increase in surprise, out-of-competition testing, but some athletes expressed concern that this would put them at a disadvantage when competing with athletes from countries that did not conduct such testing.

Another problem involved a conflict of interest. Sports governing bodies, which supervised the testing process, were aware that positive drug tests could generate bad public relations and

Olympic Testing Procedures

At the Olympics, athletes who win medals are automatically tested for performance-enhancing drugs; others may be tested at random at any time during the games. An escort notifies the athlete and accompanies him or her to the collecting station. An official watches the athlete provide the sample to ensure that it is his or her own. The urine is divided between two vials, marked A and B, and sealed. The vials are marked with a number code and sent to the lab. An International Olympic Committee (IOC) Medical Commission official keeps the list that matches the numbers to the athletes' names, but the scientists in the lab have no way of knowing whose sample they are testing.

Scientists test the A sample, while the B sample remains sealed. If the A sample tests positive for a banned drug, the lab notifies the IOC Medical Commission, which matches the code on the vial to a name on the list. The athlete is informed and given the opportunity to be present or to send a representative when the B sample is tested. If the B sample yields the same results, the lab reports this as a positive drug test. The IOC holds hearings and determines what sanctions will be imposed upon the athlete.

loss of sponsorship money. This raised questions about whether they were diligent in their efforts to identify drug-assisted athletes. Robert Voy, former USOC director of drug testing, says, "Allowing national governing bodies, international federations, and national Olympic Committees, such as the United States Olympic Committee, to govern the test-

Gold medalist Ben Johnson (right) competed in three Olympic Games before receiving a life-time ban from competition as a result of testing positive for steroid use.

ing process to ensure fair play in sport is terribly ineffective. In a sense, it is like having the fox guard the henhouse."[47]

To address the problems of conflict of interest and lack of uniformity in testing procedures, the IOC formed the World Anti-Doping Agency (WADA) in 1999. WADA coordinates and monitors antidoping efforts, including surprise, out-of-competition testing. This organization developed the World Anti-Doping Code in 2003 to ensure that all Olympic sporting federations follow the same standards. Since 2004, labs are accredited by WADA rather than by the IOC.

Problems in Professional Sports

Professional sports continue to grapple with the problems of in-house testing. Since 1990, the policy of the National Football League (NFL) has been random year-round testing, but there have been claims of positive tests being covered up, athletes being warned ahead of time that they would be tested, and athletes being able to use someone else's urine sample. Other professional sports have been criticized for lax testing programs. Major League Baseball (MLB) did not begin testing for steroids until 2003, and it tested players only once during the season. After much public pressure, the league and players' union agreed in 2005 to implement a policy allowing for random year-round tests. The National Hockey League (NHL) did not test for steroids until 2005.

The penalties imposed in professional sports for a positive drug test are not as severe as those in Olympic sports. An Olympic athlete can expect a two-year ban from his sport for a first positive test and a lifetime ban for the second. The NHL and the NBA punish a first offense with a twenty- and ten-game suspension, respectively. MLB's new policy punishes a first offense with a fifty-game suspension.

A lack of uniformity in rules also contributes to confusion. In 1998 debate arose when Mark McGwire, then the MLB single-season home run record-holder, admitted to using androstenedione, an over-the-counter supplement that converts into testosterone once it enters the body. The NFL, the IOC, and the National Collegiate Althetic Association had banned androstenedione. Because MLB had not done the same, McGwire and other players who took the supplement were not in violation of any rule. MLB added androstenedione to its list of banned substances in 2004, and in 2005 Congress made it illegal for anyone to buy, sell, or use the substance without a prescription. In another discrepancy, MLB waited until 2006 to begin testing for amphetamines, which have been outlawed by the IOC since 1967.

Designer Steroids

Even when strict rules and penalties are in place, testers wage a battle against underground chemists who develop new anabolic steroids to help athletes beat drug tests. The first clue that this was happening came in 2002, when scientists at the UCLA lab received a suspicious urine sample. They discovered that the sample contained norbolethone, an anabolic steroid that had been synthesized in 1966 but never marketed. Because labs did not expect anyone to have access to norbolethone, they were not testing for it. Catlin says, "The finding of norbolethone was really a landmark in our view, because it had to mean one of two things. Either there was a small supply of norbolethone that somebody had squirreled away for 30 or 40 years, which seemed very unlikely, or there was a chemist out there making it today."[48]

The following year an anonymous coach sent the U.S. Anti-Doping Agency (USADA) a used syringe he claimed contained a new type of anabolic steroid. USADA forwarded the substance to the UCLA lab, where scientists worked to identify it. When they put it through a mass spectrometer, the readings did not match those of any known steroid. The scientists drew diagrams in an effort to figure out the unknown molecule's structure. When they had a diagram that looked right, they synthesized the molecule, which they called tetrahydrogestrinone (THG), and put it through the mass spectrometer. The readings matched those of the substance in the syringe. "It was a brand new chemical entity that had never before been known, never been described, never patented,"[49] Catlin says.

The anonymous coach told USADA that the drug came from the Bay Area Laboratory Cooperative (BALCO), a California company that produced nutritional supplements and that was already the subject of a federal investigation. In September 2003 local and federal authorities raided BALCO's offices and found records allegedly showing that the company had supplied high-profile athletes in several sports with anabolic steroids and other illegal performance-enhancing drugs. BALCO's founder and three other men were later indicted for drug trafficking. USADA chief executive officer Terry Madden said, "What we have uncovered appears to be intentional doping of the worst sort. This is a conspiracy involving chemists, coaches, and certain athletes using what they developed to be 'undetectable' designer steroids."[50]

Fallout from the BALCO Scandal

Meanwhile, the UCLA lab worked to devise a test for THG. By mid-August 2003 international sporting federations

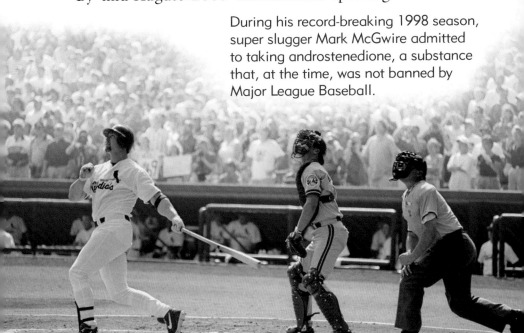

During his record-breaking 1998 season, super slugger Mark McGwire admitted to taking androstenedione, a substance that, at the time, was not banned by Major League Baseball.

began using the new test both for current competitions and to rescreen samples collected at previous competitions. Five track-and-field athletes tested positive for THG. Others who did not test positive were sanctioned when evidence collected in the BALCO investigation showed that they had used anabolic steroids and other performance-enhancing drugs. They received bans ranging from two to eight years and loss of results as far back as December 2000.

As more athletes were implicated, newspapers proclaimed the BALCO case to be the biggest sports-doping scandal in U.S. history. Four NFL players tested positive for THG. Three were fined, and the fourth had retired. In December 2004 the *San Francisco Chronicle* reported on grand jury testimony from several MLB players who, under a grant of immunity, admitted taking THG and other performance-enhancing drugs supplied by BALCO. One of these players, San Francisco Giants outfielder Barry Bonds, holds the single-

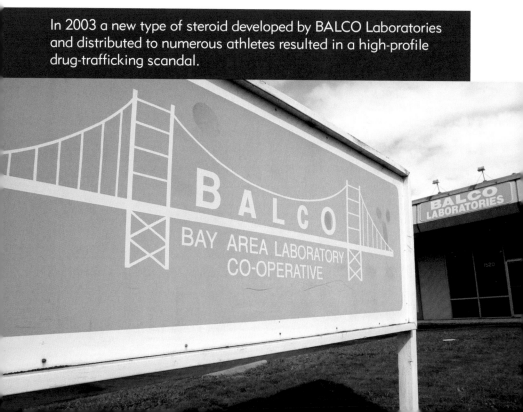

In 2003 a new type of steroid developed by BALCO Laboratories and distributed to numerous athletes resulted in a high-profile drug-trafficking scandal.

season home run record. Although Bonds claimed he did not know that the substances his trainer provided him contained anabolic steroids, the revelation generated much debate among fans as to whether his record should stand.

In the turmoil that followed the reports, MLB's drug-testing policy came under harsh criticism. The policy called for only one announced test a year, with no testing in the off-season. First-time offenders were not suspended. MLB commissioner Bud Selig promised, "I will leave no stone unturned in accomplishing our goal of zero tolerance by the start of spring training."[51] In January 2005 the league and players' union passed a new policy that included random year-round testing and a ten-game suspension for a first offense. A player would have to test positive four times before being suspended for a year. While some hailed the new policy as a step in the right direction, others proclaimed it a disappointment.

The agreement did not remove MLB from the spotlight. In a book released the following month, retired player Jose Canseco claimed that anabolic steroid use was commonplace in MLB while he was playing, and he named other players he said used the drugs. A House Government Reform Committee subpoenaed Canseco and other players to testify at a congressional hearing. The committee formed an advisory panel and indicated that its work was not done. Representative Tom Davis of Virginia said, "Today's hearing will not be the end of our inquiry. Far from it."[52]

In November 2005, under increasing pressure from Congress, MLB adopted a stricter testing policy. A first and second positive test trigger a 50- and 100-game suspension, respectively, while a third carries a lifetime ban.

While the BALCO investigation brought public awareness to the problem of performance-enhancing drugs in sports and was a victory for antidoping efforts, the existence of designer steroids presented a serious challenge. "BALCO taught us a whole lot of things that we suspected, but it then laid it right out for sport," Catlin says. "Here it is. There are lots of bad guys out there and they have all the tools. They have our methods, they have our ways, they have all our techniques."[53] Catlin believes researchers could beat underground chemists at their own game by modifying existing anabolic steroid molecules to create new ones, as the chemist who designed THG did. They could then create tests that would detect these molecules, so the tests would be in place before such a molecule shows up in a urine sample. The problem is that the amount of funding available is inadequate. To help with the fight, Catlin established the Anti-Doping Research Institute, a nonprofit organization that works to improve current testing methods and to develop new ones.

More T/E Problems and Solutions

Another BALCO product illustrates the cat-and-mouse game athletes play with drug testers. The "cream" used by athletes in the scandal is a mixture of testosterone and epitestosterone, designed to raise levels of both so the T/E ratio remains stable. Since athletes have long taken epitestosterone to get around the T/E ratio, sporting organizations limit the amount of epitestosterone an athlete can legally have in his or her urine. Catlin says, "It's another example of how there's a way to foil each and every attempt to beat the test. But it'll go on and on."[54]

Catlin developed a carbon isotope ratio test to address problems associated with the T/E ratio. Testosterone produced by the body has a different amount of carbon-13 than synthetic testosterone. By measuring carbon-13, this test answers the question of whether testosterone in a urine sample was taken from outside the body. The T/E ratio limit of 6:1 no longer applies, although the high cost of measuring the carbon isotope ratio means that all samples cannot be tested in this manner. As of 2005, WADA and the NFL both required samples with a T/E ratio above 4:1 to undergo the carbon isotope ratio test. Besides lowering the threshold for

Many baseball fans questioned the legitimacy of Barry Bonds's home-run record after the Giants outfielder admitted to taking anabolic steroids, albeit unwittingly.

cheating, the test also answers legal problems. Before this test was available, some athletes with a high T/E ratio went to court with claims that natural T/E ratios fluctuate under different circumstances.

Court Cases

Another legal issue is the possibility that an athlete's food or drink has been sabotaged by a competitor. Many athletes who test positive claim sabotage. Since sporting federations have no way to know who is lying, they follow the flat rule that the athlete is responsible for what is in his or her body. In an exceptional case, fourteen-year-old U.S. swimmer Jessica Foschi successfully fought a two-year ban after testing positive for an anabolic steroid in 1995. The unusually large

U.S. sprinter Kelli White was among those sanctioned for drug use in conjunction with the BALCO investigation. In May 2005 she testified before the U.S. Senate about the need to support antidoping efforts. White said she trained drug-free for most of her career but eventually became convinced that she needed to use performance-enhancing drugs in order to compete with other athletes who did the same.

In 2003 White won U.S. and world titles in the one-hundred-open and two-hundred-meter events. She passed seventeen drug tests while taking banned substances. In May 2004, USADA presented White with evidence collected in the BALCO investigation that showed she had used anabolic steroids and erythropoietin. She received a two-year suspension, plus the loss of all titles and results since December 2000.

At the same hearing, Don H. Catlin said, "Athletes determined to beat the system are still able to keep ahead of the game. With the paltry amount of funding currently available, antidoping research does not stand a chance."

U.S. sprinter Kelli White passed numerous drug tests while taking banned anabolic steroids.

amount of steroid in her urine, along with the fact that a medical examination turned up no evidence of anabolic steroid abuse, helped convince the court that she was the victim of sabotage.

Some court cases have dealt with the question of whether random drug testing is constitutional. For example, the parents of a seventh-grade Oregon student refused to sign a consent form allowing random drug testing, so their son was not allowed to play football. They took the case all the way to the U.S. Supreme Court on the grounds that the school's drug-testing policy violated their son's Fourth Amendment right to be free from unreasonable searches. In 1995 the Supreme Court ruled in favor of the school. In many other cases, the courts have upheld the constitutionality of random drug testing.

The Legalization Issue

The fact that drug testing has not eliminated drug use fuels another debate. Some argue that athletes will continue to use anabolic steroids and other performance-enhancing drugs and that these should be legalized. Others argue that this would undermine the meaning of athletic competition and would force all athletes to either take drugs or not be able to compete. Catlin contends:

> Legalizing drugs is not the answer. That would be a disaster because the drugs work, and they work for almost all the sports, so now there would be new records, people would run faster, they'd lift more, and they'd all be on drugs. And it would be a battle of who's got the best drugs. And the athletes would be pushed to go to the limit of how much they can take before they have some horrible side effects.[55]

Some athletes feel that they are already in this position. According to Voy, the former USOC director of drug testing:

I've had American athletes tell me they were doing performance-enhancing drugs. Most of these athletes didn't really want to do drugs. But they would come to me and say, "Unless you stop the drug abuse in sport, I have to do drugs. I'm not going to spend the next two years training—away from my family, missing my college education—to be an Olympian and then be cheated out of a medal by some guy from Europe or Asia who is on drugs."[56]

Athletes who remain drug-free feel frustrated when the public questions whether their success is due to anabolic steroid use. Some athletes welcome the opportunity to be tested to erase doubt. Before MLB passed its first drug-testing policy, New York Yankees shortstop Derek Jeter said, "Steroids are a big issue. If anything like a home run or any injury happens, people say it's steroids. That's not fair."[57] Seventy-nine percent of MLB players polled that year said that they would accept independent drug testing, and 44 percent agreed that players felt pressured to take performance-enhancing drugs to be competitive.

Perhaps the biggest obstacle to drug testing is the attitude of athletes, coaches, and chemists who rationalize the use of illegal performance-enhancing drugs. Charlie Francis, Ben Johnson's former coach, says, "I don't call it cheating. My definition of cheating is doing something nobody else is doing."[58] While newer testing methods are a frontline defense, the fight against anabolic steroid abuse must go beyond catching violators. It must also include prevention measures that target the underlying causes.

Chapter 5

A Battle on Many Fronts

The battle against anabolic steroid abuse is fought on many fronts. Lawmakers pass legislation to restrict nonprescription access to these drugs, and law enforcement officers target drug traffickers. As scientists search for answers regarding physical and psychological dependence, they develop strategies to help dependent users, although their efforts are confounded by the fact that very few users seek help. Meanwhile, prevention programs fight the problem at its source by addressing the attitudes that contribute to anabolic steroid abuse.

Closing the Prescription Loophole

In the United States before 1990, possession of anabolic steroids without a prescription was illegal in all fifty states. At that time, some physicians prescribed anabolic steroids to athletes for performance enhancement. Some were team physicians writing prescriptions for players, but others, such as a California doctor who claimed to prescribe anabolic steroids for more than ten thousand people, reasoned that it was safer for their patients to use these drugs under a doctor's supervision than to self-administer black-market drugs.

Even so, by the 1980s most users obtained their anabolic steroids from the black market rather than from a physician. In 1984 narcotics agents arrested Charles J. Radler, whose million-dollar-a-year operation made him the biggest anabolic steroid dealer in the United States. Radler explained how his business had grown rapidly in only a few months:

> I couldn't keep up with it. I thought there were a few weightlifters in a few weight rooms who used steroids. Then I started to find out: *Everybody* uses steroids. It's the bodybuilders, the powerlifters, it's about every sport there is. I started getting calls from college football teams. That surprised me at first. Now it would surprise me if there was a college football team out there that isn't using steroids.[59]

Radler was convicted on eighteen counts of illegally selling prescription drugs and one count of racketeering. He was sentenced to one to two years in jail and was fined $115,000.

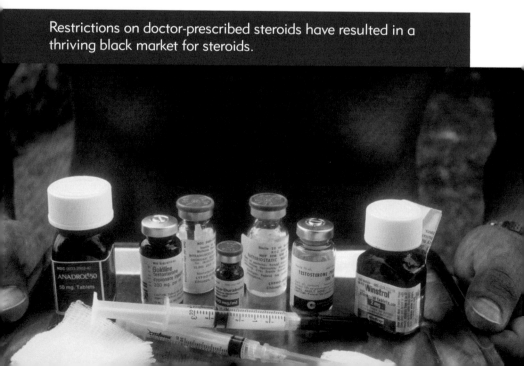

Restrictions on doctor-prescribed steroids have resulted in a thriving black market for steroids.

The Anabolic Steroid Control Act of 1990 reclassified anabolic steroids as a Schedule III controlled substance, putting them in the same category as ketamine (Special K), certain barbiturates, and LSD precursors. The new classification means increased penalties for anabolic steroid traffickers, plus forfeiture of property and profits related to the sale of these drugs. For a first offense, simple possession carries a penalty of up to a year in prison and/or a maximum fine of $5,000, and trafficking carries a penalty of up to five years in prison and a maximum fine of $250,000. In both cases, the penalty doubles for the second offense.

Classification of anabolic steroids as a controlled substance also means that physicians are limited to prescribing these drugs for treatment of disease. A few physicians are willing to risk breaking the law. In one 2005 case, an endocrinologist in Texas lost his license and was fined $190,000 for prescribing anabolic steroids to athletes. In some cases, human users get the drugs from veterinarians who prescribe them for animals. An estimated 10 to 15 percent of illegal users get their anabolic steroids with a prescription.

An International Black Market

The remaining illegal users support an international black market with sales estimated at $500 million to $1 billion a year. Most black-market anabolic steroids sold in the United States are smuggled in from other countries. In Mexico anabolic steroids can be purchased legally over the counter. Users and traffickers cross the border, buy the drugs, and smuggle them back into the United States. Some Mexican pharmacies pay couriers to smuggle the drugs into the United States and then mail them to U.S. customers.

In 2004 the Drug Enforcement Administration (DEA) noted that groups of Russian, Romanian, and Greek nationals were smuggling large amounts of anabolic steroids into the United States. Black-market steroids also come from other European countries, South America, and Canada.

Canadian law enforcement efforts have decreased the amount of steroids smuggled from Canada into the United States. In most other countries, however, these drugs are not regulated, which makes it impossible to fight the problem at its source.

Some anabolic steroids produced legally in the United States end up on the black market. In these cases, pharmacists, physicians, veterinarians, pharmaceutical company employees, or others with access to legal supplies sell them illegally. Other supplies are manufactured in clandestine laboratories. These counterfeit steroids are packaged like those produced by licensed pharmaceutical companies, but many are simply a mixture of vegetable oil and alcohol and contain no anabolic steroid. Some contain only a small amount of an anabolic steroid, which may not be the same type named on the package. Because counterfeit steroids are not manufactured under sterile conditions, they pose additional dangers to users.

Resourceful Traffickers

FBI special agent Gregory Stejskal noted that dealers get away with selling fake anabolic steroids because many users practice stacking, or using more than one anabolic steroid at a time. The dealer sells both genuine and fake steroids to the same user. The results the user experiences from the genuine steroids blind him or her to the fact that some of the products contain no active ingredient. Stejskal says that dealers "can increase sales or help their business even further by acting as 'consultants,' advising the users which combination of steroids to take."[60]

A Michigan dealer who sold both genuine and fake anabolic steroids serves as an example. He purchased the same types of bottles and caps used by licensed pharmaceutical companies and hired a professional printer to produce labels, boxes, and package inserts. He used a computer program to duplicate the formats that various pharmaceutical manufacturers use to print their lot numbers and expiration dates on the labels. He then filled the counterfeit packages with fake

SCHEDULE OF CONTROLLED SUBSTANCES

Rating	Examples	Characteristics
Schedule I	· Heroin · Mescaline · LSD · MDMA (Ecstasy) · Marijuana · PCP · GHB · Methaqualone · Psilocybin (mushrooms)	High potential for abuse; no currently accepted medical use in the United States.
Schedule II	· Opium and Opiates · Methamphetamines · Demerol · Percodan · Cocaine · Amphetamines · Oxycodone · Hydrocodone	High potential for abuse; currently accepted medical use with severe restrictions.
Schedule III	· Anabolic steroids · Codeine · Certain barbiturates · Ketamine (Special K)	Potential for abuse, but less than Schedule I and II substances; currently accepted medical use.
Schedule IV	· Certain barbiturates · Benzodiazepines (Sleeping pills)	Less potential for abuse; available by prescription.
Schedule V	· Cold and cough medicines	Least potential for abuse; available over the counter.

steroids that he produced. He was among more than forty people from the United States, Canada, and Mexico indicted in 1992 as part of a joint Federal Bureau of Investigation–Food and Drug Administration undercover operation.

Dealers sell black-market anabolic steroids in gyms and locker rooms, at bodybuilding and weight-lifting competitions, through mail-order businesses, and over the Internet. The Internet auction site eBay has security filters to prevent auctions of illegal products, but some anabolic steroid dealers found a creative way around the filters. Until the problem came to light in 2004, these dealers listed their products as books or pamphlets about steroids but sent the actual drugs to winning bidders.

Traffickers also use Internet pharmacies to sell their wares. In April 2005 authorities in the United States and four other countries arrested twenty people in the culmination of a joint investigation called Operation Cyber Chase. The traffickers had used more than two hundred Web sites to distribute controlled substances. DEA administrator Karen P. Tandy says,

"For too long the Internet has been an open medicine cabinet with cyber drug dealers illegally doling out a vast array of narcotics, amphetamines, and steroids. In this first major international enforcement action against online rogue pharmacies and their sources of supply, we've logged these traffickers off the Internet."[61]

Expanded Efforts

Earlier in 2005 the DEA set up a toll-free international hotline to fight prescription drug trafficking and abuse. The public can call 1-877-RxAbuse to anonymously report such activity. By April 2005 the DEA had already received hundreds of calls.

Congress stepped up the fight by adding anabolic steroid precursors such as androstenedione to the list of Schedule III controlled substances. Until the new law took effect in January 2005, these products, which convert into testosterone after they enter the body, were sold legally as over-the-counter diet supplements. Once Congress passed the new law, users rushed to stock up on remaining supplies before the ban went into effect.

The battle against anabolic steroid abuse is a challenge for law enforcement since personnel are often overtaxed with fighting other drugs of abuse, such as cocaine and heroin, that are considered more harmful than steroids. In addition, U.S. sentencing guidelines base penalties on the amount of dosage units involved. Since these guidelines define a dosage unit of anabolic steroids as a much larger amount than users normally take, most users and small-scale dealers would receive only a light penalty if convicted. Law enforcement agents concentrate their efforts on large-scale anabolic steroid traffickers, who can receive higher penalties.

Symptoms of Physical Dependence

Adding to the complexity of the battle is the fact that many users seem to become dependent on the drugs. Other drugs,

In July 2003 Taylor Hooton, a seventeen-year-old high school baseball player from Plano, Texas, committed suicide. His parents believe this was triggered by anabolic steroid withdrawal depression. In retrospect, they realize that Taylor showed virtually all of the classic signs of anabolic steroid abuse. He gained thirty pounds of muscle in a few months and developed severe acne on his back, oily skin, puffiness in the neck and face, and bad breath. Although he had no history of behavioral or emotional problems, he began to exhibit severe mood swings and would fly into rages. When his parents became suspicious, they confronted Taylor, who denied using anabolic steroids.

After Taylor's death, his family and friends learned that anabolic steroid abuse is growing among high school students, who are generally unaware of the dangers. They founded the Taylor Hooton Foundation for Fighting Steroid Abuse (THF) to educate students, parents, and coaches about the dangers, the warning signs, and what to do when they discover that a friend or loved one is abusing anabolic steroids. Taylor's experience, along with the tragic experiences of others, is posted on the THF Web site, www.taylorhooton.org.

Donald Hooton, whose son used steroids in high school, established a foundation to educate young people about the dangers of steroid abuse.

such as cocaine and heroin, produce dependence by acting on the reward centers in the brain. Unlike these drugs, anabolic steroids do not produce an immediate "high," although some users report feeling pleasure from taking them over a period of time. Scientists debate whether anabolic steroids produce this pleasure by acting on the brain or whether users feel rewarded because they enjoy their increased muscle size and strength.

The effect of anabolic steroids on natural testosterone production can cause withdrawal symptoms associated with physical dependence. When users take anabolic steroids, thus raising their levels higher than normal, the pituitary gland signals the testes to stop producing testosterone. The testes gradually shrink. When users stop taking anabolic steroids, it may be several weeks before their testes return to normal size and resume production. Meanwhile, users experience temporary hypogonadism, a state in which their testosterone levels are abnormally low. During this state, some users experience hormonal-induced depression. Harrison G. Pope Jr. of McLean Hospital says, "The first thing they want to do is to go back on the steroids so that they feel decent again. And so there is some biological tendency that encourages these guys to go back on over and over again."[62]

Withdrawal depression usually goes away once natural testosterone levels return to normal, but some users have remained depressed for months. Case reports exist of depressed users who committed suicide when they tried to go off the drugs.

Psychological Dependence—Never Big Enough

Many users also exhibit psychological dependence because they cannot face the idea of losing their steroid-induced muscle gains. Former NFL defensive end Lyle Alzado explained why he took anabolic steroids almost continuously from 1969 until 1991, several years after his retirement: "It was addicting, mentally addicting. I just didn't feel strong unless I was taking something."[63]

The experience of Larry Pacifico, who won nine consecutive powerlifting world titles, illustrates the pull anabolic steroids can have on users. In 1981, at age thirty-five, he was diagnosed with advanced coronary artery disease. He and his doctor believed anabolic steroids were one of the contributing factors. Pacifico says, "Steroids aren't a part of my life now, but I'd be lying if I said I didn't miss them. And you know what? I may even take them again because I may not be able to *keep* myself from taking them."[64]

These experiences seem to contradict the fact that many professional athletes apparently have no trouble stopping anabolic steroid use when they retire. This led some researchers to conclude that psychological dependence may hinge in part on the reason a person uses anabolic steroids. Athletes who view these drugs simply as tools to improve performance may no longer feel a need to use them when their athletic careers end. Users driven by a desire to improve their body image may be distressed by the thought of becoming smaller or weaker should they stop.

Scott Genslinger, a twenty-eight-year-old bodybuilder who spent thousands of dollars on anabolic steroids and other growth drugs, gives insight into this type of thinking: "It was an addiction. The way doctors described it to me, it was similar to anorexia nervosa—except you have an obsession with being big instead of being skinny. When I was off steroids, I was afraid to step on a scale for fear I might have lost weight. If I missed a meal, I went totally nuts. It ruined my day."[65]

This disorder was once called reverse anorexia nervosa. In 1997 researchers at Harvard Medical School proposed replacing this term with *muscle dysmorphia* to describe a disorder in which people believe they are small and weak when in reality they are big and muscular. People with this disorder may become so preoccupied with their muscularity that they forego social invitations or give up personal relationships and careers in order to spend more time at the gym. They often wear long sleeves or baggy clothing to hide their bodies, and they avoid beaches, pools, locker rooms, and other places where their bodies would be exposed. Muscle dysmorphia, which appears to be much more common among men than among women, may lead to dependence on anabolic steroids and other muscle-building drugs.

Additionally, anabolic steroids may contribute to new cases of muscle dysmorphia. Once a user increases his muscle size with anabolic steroids, he may not feel muscular enough without them. One such user told the Harvard researchers, "Why should I go back to being Clark Kent when I can be Superman?"[66] Bodybuilding magazines, movies, and advertisements display men who are muscular to a degree not possible without the use of anabolic steroids. Men who

Bodybuilders can develop a psychological dependence on steroids once they experience the accelerated results of taking the drug.

compare themselves with these images may feel dissatisfied with their appearance. Even some children's toys help send the message that extreme muscularity is the ideal. A study that compared action figures produced over a thirty-year period revealed that the figures had become increasingly muscular. Many of the newer figures resemble advanced bodybuilders, and others have a muscle size impossible for humans to achieve.

Challenges to Treatment

Researchers do not know what percentage of anabolic steroid users become physically or psychologically dependent. Studies attempting to measure dependence rates have yielded results ranging from 14 to 69 percent of study subjects. This contrasts with the low percentage of users seeking treatment. Pope says, "I could count on both hands the number of patients who have sought treatment from me for [addiction to] steroids."[67] A 1992 study estimated that of the patients entering drug treatment programs in a recent year, less than 0.1 percent (forty-one patients) used anabolic steroids. Only one of these was seeking treatment for anabolic steroid dependence; the others were seeking help for dependence on drugs they were taking at the same time as anabolic steroids.

Dependent users may be disinclined to seek treatment for a variety of reasons. Many do not consider themselves dependent since anabolic steroids do not cause the high associated with other drugs of abuse. Others fear the consequences of admitting illegal drug use or enjoy the admiration they receive for their physiques. Pope and Kirk J. Brower believe that society's emphasis on muscularity, as seen in both the media and the evolution of children's action figures, encourages users to view anabolic steroid use in a favorable light. They write, "We think nothing of seeing an advertisement promoting a powerful car or truck as being 'on steroids,' whereas no one would advertise the same vehicle as being 'on cocaine' or 'on marijuana.'"[68]

Some dependent users may be able to stop on their own, but others need professional help. Few treatment programs exist that specifically target anabolic steroid dependence, and few doctors are experienced in treating it. Since anabolic steroids differ from other drugs of abuse, experts recommend that doctors understand the reasons the patient used anabolic steroids and help him or her find alternatives, such as a nutrition or exercise program with realistic goals. Doctors should also explain the withdrawal symptoms the patient may experience and should monitor him or her during this time. If the patient becomes severely depressed during withdrawal or if the symptoms last for several weeks, doctors may prescribe antidepressants, although this does not seem to be necessary with most patients. Experts recommend hospitalization in extreme cases, such as when a patient becomes suicidal or violent or has been unable to stop anabolic steroid use as an outpatient.

The Role of Attitudes

Besides keeping dependent users from recognizing their problem, the lack of a negative perception toward anabolic steroid use also hampers prevention efforts. Potential users often associate anabolic steroids with such positive factors as improved appearance, athletic success, fame, admiration, and financial rewards. Dutch track coach Henk Kraayenhof says, "People like to think that things are better since Ben Johnson. I argue the opposite. If anything, Ben Johnson's getting caught promoted drug use. He won."[69]

Don H. Catlin, head of the UCLA lab accredited by the World Anti-Doping Agency, would like to "shift the culture" by rewarding athletes who remain drug-free. He is trying to find financial support for a volunteer program in which athletes who sign up would be able to prove that they are drug-free by agreeing to be tested anywhere, day or night. Doctors would also monitor volunteers' biomarkers, such as blood pressure, cholesterol, and testosterone levels to determine what readings are normal for the athlete. If one of these biomarkers

As founder and head instructor of Team Conditioning Systems, Gregory "Graig" White designs natural performance-enhancing training programs for athletes at all levels, beginning in high school. According to White, who is also the director of performance enhancement at Rutgers University, high school athletes considering anabolic steroids should think about two questions. The first is: "Steroids are effective, but at what cost?" The detrimental effects on body and mind, along with the high cost of potential medical bills, moved him to conclude: "From where I sit, there is no good reason I can think of for a high school athlete to venture into this world."

The second question is: "If you look at it in real numbers how many athletes in high school are actually taking steroids?" Some young athletes feel tempted to take anabolic steroids because they believe that most of their competitors are doing the same. Although polls show that high school use is growing, they also show that the vast majority of high school students have never tried anabolic steroids. White believes that high school athletes who use "a sound training protocol" will come out on top.

Besides sound training, White mentions two important components of athletic success that young athletes often neglect. "The thing I have found most prevalent in high school athletes is the fact that most of them eat horribly." The other component is rest. Some athletes overtrain out of fear of falling behind, but "rest is something everyone needs and my athletes will tell you that they get plenty of it," White says.

suddenly changed, doctors would try to find a natural explanation. If they determined that the athlete was doping, that athlete would lose public standing as a program member, although he or she would not be suspended from competition. Catlin explains: "As long as you stay clean, you keep getting stars next to your name, and your name will be published; you're on our clean list. And if you fumble the ball and have a positive test, you're out of the program."[70] He hopes such a program would promote a drug-free attitude.

Charles E. Yesalis of Penn State University blames much of the problem on the win-at-all-costs attitude evident in society and promoted by some coaches and parents. He says, "If you really teach your kid to win at all costs, I think drug use is exquisitely rational." He notes that some athletes may be unwilling to accept the idea of giving up an unfair edge to others who use anabolic steroids:

> I've been asked a number of times, "Dr. Yesalis, can you get bigger and stronger and better-conditioned training without drugs?" Yes, you can. Pretty much from eight to eighty. But that's not the tough question. "Can you get as big and as strong and as well-conditioned training naturally as you can on drugs?" Absolutely not. Mom and Dad, accept it, get used to it. Kid, accept it, get used to it. Coach, accept it, get used to it.[71]

Alternatives to Anabolic Steroid Use

When young athletes fail to make athletic gains through natural means, often the problem is an improper diet or a lack of understanding of strength-training principles. Education in these areas could help prevent such athletes from turning to anabolic steroids. Thomas W. Storer, an exercise physiologist at UCLA, advises young athletes:

> First and foremost, if I wanted to increase athletic performance, I would develop the best training program

Education programs designed to teach students about proper nutrition and training are on the rise in an effort to combat steroid use among young athletes.

that I could, and I would seek out advice for that. I would find a trainer who could help me realize the best that I could be with training. And I would work with a dietitian, someone who could help optimize the nutritional support of this exercise training program.[72]

In this way, athletes can attain lasting benefits rather than steroid-induced gains that disappear when they stop taking the drugs.

Researchers at the Oregon Health Sciences University (OHSU) recognized the need to teach these principles when they observed the ineffectiveness of some traditional prevention strategies. For example, when they presented student athletes with information on both the risks and the benefits of anabolic steroid use, they found that the students' attitudes toward these drugs did not change. They next tried presenting only the negative effects of anabolic steroids and found that this increased some students' interest in taking the drugs.

Using what they had discovered, the OHSU researchers developed Athletes Training and Learning to Avoid Steroids (ATLAS). This program, which was launched in 1993, is presented to male high school athletes in a team setting and includes sessions in the classroom and in the weight room. Participants learn weight-training skills and principles of sports nutrition, including how to meet training needs through a proper diet rather than by using supplements or performance-enhancing drugs. They also learn the facts about anabolic steroids and practice skills to resist drug offers.

To test the effectiveness of ATLAS, researchers conducted a study in which they compared high school football teams

Additional Reasons to Train Naturally

Young athletes who take anabolic steroids as a shortcut to muscularity may fail to develop other components of athletic success. Exercise physiologist Thomas D. Fahey says, "The key to athletic success is developing basic sports skills and fitness, and if you rely on drugs to do this, you'll never reach the level of competence that you need to become either a successful athlete or competent in recreational sports."

University of Iowa wrestling coach Dan Gable, quoted in Charles E. Yesalis and Virginia S. Cowart's book *The Steroids Game*, identifies another edge that must be developed naturally: "Besides the health effects, what you lose when you use steroids is mental toughness. The key to victory is that the strongest mind wins. You can get physical strength with steroids, but you lose the mental toughness it took to get to a high level naturally."

that went through the program with teams that received only a pamphlet about anabolic steroids. A year after the program, the group that received the pamphlet had twice as many new anabolic steroid users as the ATLAS group. Compared to the other group, the ATLAS-trained athletes reported better nutrition and exercise habits, less desire to begin anabolic steroid use, and greater belief in their vulnerability to harm from anabolic steroids. They also reported less new use of alcohol and other illicit drugs (marijuana, amphetamines, and narcotics).

The positive results from ATLAS led to the formation of a similar program for young female athletes in 1999. Athletes Targeting Healthy Exercise and Nutrition Alternatives (ATHENA) addresses drug abuse and disordered eating and teaches nutrition and exercise skills. Researchers analyzing the short-term results found that participants used fewer body-image drugs, including anabolic steroids, practiced better eating habits, and reported fewer injuries and less sexual activity. They are still analyzing the long-term results.

The success of the ATLAS and ATHENA programs indicates that anabolic steroid abuse can be prevented, but the problem is unlikely to disappear anytime soon. The number of scandals in the headlines—and the rationalization by those involved in the scandals—indicates that many will continue to turn to anabolic steroids and other illegal drugs to gain a competitive edge. A 1983 statement by Arnold Beckett of the International Olympic Committee Medical Commission remains timely: "What we must always remember is this. It is a never-ending process." Beckett made a case for continuing the fight despite the overwhelming nature of the problem. He did not believe that drug use among athletes would be eradicated, but he did believe that scientists could continue to reduce the level of doping, thus promoting fairness and health. He concluded, "That's our job. Consider the alternative."[73]

NOTES

Introduction: An Ongoing Scandal

1. Quoted in Bil Gilbert, "Problems in a Turned-On World," *Sports Illustrated*, June 23, 1969, p. 67.
2. Quoted in CNN, "McGwire Mum on Steroids in Hearing," March 17, 2005. www.cnn.com/2005/ALLPOLITICS/03/17/steroids.baseball/index.html.
3. Quoted in CNN, "McGwire Mum on Steroids in Hearing."
4. Jack Curry, "Steroids Taint Baseball's Big Bang," *New York Times*, August 17, 2005. www.nytimes.com/2005/08/17/sports/baseball/17homeruns.html?ex=1127448000&en=dbc636131b31e885&ei=5070.
5. Don H. Catlin, interview with the author, April 2005.
6. George W. Bush, "Transcript of State of the Union," CNN, January 21, 2004. www.cnn.com/2004/ALLPOLITICS/01/20/sotu.transcript.5/index.html.
7. Quoted in *McLaughlin Group*, transcript for March 18, 2005. www.mclaughlin.com/library/transcript.asp?id=458.
8. Quoted in Gilbert, "Problems in a Turned-On World," p. 67.

Chapter 1: The Quest for Strength

9. Quoted in Charles E. Yesalis, ed., *Anabolic Steroids in Sport and Exercise*, 2nd ed. Champaign, IL: Human Kinetics, 2000, p. 53.
10. Quoted in Terry Todd, "The Steroid Predicament," *Sports Illustrated*, August 1, 1983, p. 66.
11. Quoted in Gilbert, "Problems in a Turned-On World," p. 66.
12. Quoted in Yesalis, ed., *Anabolic Steroids in Sport and Exercise*, p. 55.

13. Quoted in Steve Courson and Lee. R. Schreiber, *False Glory*. Stamford, CT: Longmeadow, 1991, p. 150.
14. Quoted in Courson and Schreiber, *False Glory*, p. 57.
15. Quoted in William Oscar Johnson, "Steroids: A Problem of Huge Dimensions," *Sports Illustrated*, May 13, 1985, p. 42.
16. Courson and Schreiber, *False Glory*, p. 17.

Chapter 2: Use and Abuse of a Muscle-Building Drug

17. Shalender Bhasin, interview with the author, December 2004.
18. Quoted in Werner W. Franke and Brigitte Berendonk, "Hormonal Doping and Androgenization of Athletes: A Secret Program of the German Democratic Republic Government," *Clinical Chemistry*, 1997, p. 1264.
19. Quoted in Bil Gilbert, "Something Extra on the Ball," *Sports Illustrated*, June 30, 1969, p. 42.
20. Courson and Schreiber, *False Glory*, p. 26.
21. Thomas D. Fahey, interview with the author, December 2004.
22. Bhasin, interview.
23. Fahey, interview.
24. Bhasin, interview.
25. Bhasin, interview.
26. David B. Allen, "Growth Effects of Inhaled Corticosteroids: Straight Stories or Tall Tales?" Medscape, 2002. www.medscape.com.

Chapter 3: Success with a Price

27. Quoted in Franke and Berendonk, "Hormonal Doping and Adrogenization of Athletes," p. 1274.
28. Quoted in Franke and Berendonk, "Hormonal Doping and Androgenization of Athletes," p. 1273.
29. Charles E. Yesalis, interview with the author, December 2004.
30. Quoted in Paul Zimmerman, "The Agony Must End," *Sports Illustrated*, November 10, 1986, p. 18.

31. Charles E. Yesalis, interview with the author, June 2005.

32. Fahey, interview.

33. Steve Courson, e-mail interview with the author, April 2005.

34. Lyle Alzado, "I'm Sick and I'm Scared," *Sports Illustrated*, July 8, 1991, p. 21.

35. Quoted in Alzado, "I'm Sick and I'm Scared," p. 23.

36. Harrison G. Pope Jr., interview with the author, May 2005.

37. Thomas W. Storer, interview with the author, December 2004.

38. Quoted in Yesalis, *Anabolic Steroids in Sport and Exercise*, p. 265.

39. Bhasin, interview.

40. Pope, interview.

41. Quoted in *New York Times*, "Steroid Use Goes on Trial," April 2, 1986, p. A22.

42. Yesalis, interview, December 2004.

Chapter 4: A Game of Cat and Mouse

43. Quoted in Terry Todd, "Anabolic Steroids: The Gremlins of Sport," *Journal of Sport History*, Spring 1987, p. 90.

44. Quoted in Craig Neff, "Caracas: A Scandal and a Warning," *Sports Illustrated*, September 5, 1983, p. 19.

45. Catlin, interview.

46. Quoted in Jere Longman, "U.S.O.C. Experts Call Drug Testing a Failure," *New York Times*, April 9, 1995, p. S11.

47. Quoted in Charles E. Yesalis and Virginia S. Cowart, *The Steroids Game*. Champaign, IL: Human Kinetics, 1998, p. 178.

48. Catlin, interview.

49. Catlin, interview.

50. Quoted in David Wharton, "Breaking the Code," *Los Angeles Times*, November 6, 2003, p. D9.

51. Quoted in Bill Saporito, "How Pumped Up Is Baseball?" *Time*, December 13, 2004, p. 34.

52. Quoted in Alex Kingsbury, "Throwing Some Heat," *U.S. News & World Report*, March 28, 2005, p. 41.

53. Catlin, interview.
54. Catlin, interview.
55. Catlin, interview.
56. Quoted in Michael Bamberger and Don Yaeger, "Over the Edge," *Sports Illustrated*, April 14, 1997, p. 63.
57. Quoted in Mel Antonen, "*USA Today* Poll: 79% of Players Want Drug Testing," *USA Today*, July 8, 2002, p. 1A.
58. Quoted in Merrell Noden, ed., "A Dirty System," *Sports Illustrated*, December 17, 1990, p. 27.

Chapter 5: A Battle on Many Fronts

59. Quoted in Johnson, "Steroids," p. 61.
60. Gregory Stejskal, "They Shoot Horses, Don't They? Anabolic Steroids and Their Challenge to Law Enforcement," *FBI Law Enforcement Bulletin*, August 1994, pp. 1–6.
61. Quoted in *Drug Enforcement Administration*, "International Drug Ring Shattered," April 20, 2005. www.usdoj.gov/dea.
62. Pope, interview.
63. Alzado, "I'm Sick and I'm Scared," p. 24.
64. Quoted in Todd, "The Steroid Predicament," p. 70.
65. Quoted in Johnson, "Steroids," p. 49.
66. Quoted in Harrison G. Pope Jr. et al., "Muscle Dysmorphia: An Underrecognized Form of Body Dysmorphic Disorder," *Psychosomatics*, vol. 38, 1997, p. 553.
67. Quoted in Jerry Adler, "Toxic Strength," *Newsweek*, December 20, 2004, p. 46.
68. Harrison G. Pope Jr. and Kirk J. Brower, "Anabolic-Androgenic Steroids," in *The American Psychiatric Publishing Textbook of Substance Abuse Treatment*, 3rd ed., ed. Marc Galanter and Herbert D. Kleber. Washington, DC: American Psychiatric, 2004, p. 257.
69. Quoted in Bamberger and Yaeger, "Over the Edge," p. 70.
70. Catlin, interview.
71. Yesalis, interview, December 2004.
72. Storer, interview.
73. Quoted in Todd, "The Steroid Predicament," p. 76.

ORGANIZATIONS TO CONTACT

National Clearinghouse for Alcohol and Drug Information (NCADI)
PO Box 2345, Rockville, MD 20847-2345
(800) 729-6686
www.health.org

The NCADI provides publications, posters, and videocassettes on substance abuse prevention and treatment. Some resources are available online; others can be ordered for no or low cost over the phone. Callers can also ask questions about prevention and treatment twenty-four hours a day.

National Federation of State High School Associations (NFHS)
PO Box 690, Indianapolis, IN 46206
(317) 972-6900
www.nfhs.org

The NFHS serves high school athletic/activity associations in the United States. To address anabolic steroid abuse in high schools, the NFHS offers an educational program that includes videos, brochures, and posters for use by students, parents, and coaches.

National Institute on Drug Abuse (NIDA)
6001 Executive Blvd., Bethesda, MD 20892-9561
(888) 644-6432
(301) 443-1124
www.steroidabuse.org

In 2000 NIDA launched a Web site dedicated to teaching the public about the dangers of anabolic steroid abuse. Information on other drugs of abuse can be found through NIDA's home page (www.drugabuse.gov).

Office of National Drug Control Policy (ONDCP)
Drug Policy Information Clearinghouse
PO Box 6000, Rockville, MD 20849-6000
(800) 666-3332
www.whitehousedrugpolicy.gov

The ONDCP writes the nation's strategy for fighting abuse, trafficking, and other activities related to illegal drugs. Its Web site provides facts and figures on many illegal drugs, including anabolic steroids.

Taylor Hooton Foundation for Fighting Steroid Abuse (THF)
6009 W. Parker Rd., Suite 148, PMB Box 138, Plano, Texas 75093
(877) 503-7300
(972) 403-7300
www.taylorhooton.org

Founded in memory of Taylor Hooton, this foundation seeks to educate the public about the dangers of anabolic steroid abuse and emphasizes prevention among young people. The THF Web site provides educational resources and shares the tragic experiences of users and their families.

United States Anti-Doping Agency (USADA)
2550 Tenderfoot Hill St., Suite 200, Colorado Springs, CO 80906-7346
(866) 601-2632
(719) 785-2000
www.usantidoping.org

USADA is the official antidoping organization for the U.S. Olympic Movement. Its Web site provides educational materials to help both student and elite athletes train and compete successfully without drugs.

FOR FURTHER READING

Books

Steve Courson and Lee R. Schreiber, *False Glory*. Stamford, CT: Longmeadow, 1991. Former NFL offensive lineman Steve Courson details his experiences in the NFL and with anabolic steroids, including the repercussions of speaking up about steroid use.

Cynthia Kuhn, Scott Swartzwelder, and Wilkie Wilson, *Pumped: Straight Facts for Athletes About Drugs, Supplements, and Training*. New York: W.W. Norton, 2000. The authors explain the science behind how the body works and how a variety of drugs, including anabolic steroids, stimulants, diet supplements, and recreational drugs, affect health and athletic performance.

Harrison G. Pope Jr., Katharine A. Phillips, and Roberto Olivardia, *The Adonis Complex: The Secret Crisis of Male Body Obsession*. New York: The Free Press, 2000. The authors employ their experiences with patients and research subjects to weave an engaging discussion of muscle dysmorphia and other body-image disorders. They examine the role anabolic steroids play in this growing problem, offer coping strategies, and provide tests that readers can take to see if they suffer from a body-image disorder.

Thomas M. Santella, *Body Enhancement Products*. Philadelphia: Chelsea House, 2005. This book discusses a wide spectrum of performance-enhancing drugs and methods, explaining the reasons athletes and others use them, how they work, and the associated risks. It also examines issues regarding teen use, drug testing, and drug control.

Web Sites

Oregon Health & Science University (ohsu.edu). The home of the ATLAS and ATHENA programs gives an overview of their components and results.

Play True (www.wada-ama.org). The official magazine of the World Anti-Doping Agency (WADA) reports on current programs and activities, examines issues related to doping, and presents athlete profiles. All issues can be downloaded from the WADA Web site.

Periodicals

Jerry Adler, "Toxic Strength," *Newsweek*, December 20, 2004.

Lyle Alzado, "I'm Sick and I'm Scared," *Sports Illustrated*, July 8, 1991.

———, "*USA Today* Poll: 79% of Players Want Drug Testing," *USA Today*, July 8, 2002.

Michael Bamberger and Don Yaeger, "Over the Edge," *Sports Illustrated*, April 14, 1997.

Werner W. Franke and Brigitte Berendonk, "Hormonal Doping and Androgenization of Athletes: A Secret Program of the German Democratic Republic Government," *Clinical Chemistry*, 1997.

Bil Gilbert, "Problems in a Turned-On World," *Sports Illustrated*, June 23, 1969.

———, "Something Extra on the Ball," *Sports Illustrated*, June 30, 1969.

Houston Chronicle, "Doctor Loses License over Steroids for Bodybuilders," February 8, 2005.

Alex Kingsbury, "Throwing Some Heat," *U.S. News & World Report*, March 28, 2005.

Jere Longman, "East German Steroids' Toll: 'They Killed Heidi,'" *New York Times*, January 26, 2004.

Harrison G. Pope Jr. and Gen Kanayama, "Abuse of Anabolic-Androgenic Steroids," *Pharmaceutical News*, vol. 7, no. 5, 2000.

Bill Saporito, "How Pumped Up Is Baseball?" *Time*, December 13, 2004.

Mark Starr, "High and Inside," *Newsweek*, December 13, 2004.

Internet Sources

Associated Press, "Girls Are Abusing Steroids, Too," *USA Today*, April 25, 2005. www.usatoday.com/news/health/2005-04-25-girls-steroids_x.htm?csp=34.

BBC News, "GDR Athletes Sue over Steroid Damage," March 13, 2005. http://news.bbc.co.uk/2/hi/europe/4341045.stm.

Mike Brunker, "Steroid Dealers Use Ruse to Sell Wares on eBay," MSNBC, January 20, 2005. www.msnbc.msn.com/id/6809149

Don H. Catlin, "Statement of Don H. Catlin, M.D. to the U.S. Senate Commerce Committee," U.S. Senate Committee on Commerce, Science & Transportation, May 24, 2005. http://commerce.senate.gov/hearings/testimony.cfm?id=1511&wit_id=4278.

CNN, "McGwire Mum on Steroids in Hearing," March 17, 2005. www.cnn.com/2005/ALLPOLITICS/03/17/steroids.baseball/index.html.

Jack Curry, "Steroids Taint Baseball's Big Bang," *New York Times,* August 17, 2005. www.nytimes.com/2005/08/17/sports/baseball/17homeruns.html?ex=1127448000&en=dbc636131 b31e885&ei=5070.

John Donovan, "A First Step," *Sports Illustrated,* January 13, 2005. http://sportsillustrated.cnn.com/2005/writers/ john_donovan/01/13/steroids.qa/index.htm.

Drug Enforcement Administration Diversion Control Program, "Anabolic Steroids—Hidden Dangers," March 2004. www.deadiversion.usdoj.gov/pubs/brochures/steroids/hidden/index.htm.

McLaughlin Group, transcript for March 18, 2005. www.mclaughlin.com/library/transcript.asp?id=458.

National Institute on Drug Abuse, "Steroids (Anabolic-Androgenic)," April 2000. www.nida.nih.gov/Infofacts/Steroids. html.

Sal Ruibal, "Tackling Longtime Issue of Drugs No. 2 on Sports Changes Wish List," *USA Today,* September 9, 2004. www.usatoday.com/sports/2004-09-09-ten-changes-drugs-testing_x.htm.

USA Today, "BALCO Glance and Glossary," May 20, 2005. www.usatoday.com/sports/balco-glance.htm.

Kelli White, "Statement of Kelli White," U.S. Senate Committee on Commerce, Science & Transportation, May 24, 2005. http://commerce.senate.gov/hearings/testimony.cfm?id=115 &wit_id=4276.

INDEX

PICTURE CREDITS

ABOUT THE AUTHOR

Jacqueline Adams has loved writing since she was four years old. She began her career as a freelance writer in 2000. Since then, many of her articles and short stories have appeared in Cricket Magazine Group publications, *Science World*, *Highlights for Children*, *Odyssey*, *Read*, and other magazines. Her work won the *Highlights for Children* Fiction Contest in both 2003 and 2005 and the Society of Children's Book Writers and Illustrators (SCBWI) Magazine Merit Award for Nonfiction in 2004. She serves on the Board of Advisors for the Western Pennsylvania SCBWI and edits its newsletter, *The Golden Penn*.

Adams encounters ideas for stories when traveling with her husband, son, and daughter. The family enjoys hiking, camping, and canoeing in the forests of Pennsylvania and spending time with their dogs and cat.